Fear Is Not My Boss!

Fear IS NOT My Boss!

To Weather the Storm

SONYA R. WARD

Life Channels Vessel to Vessel Publishing **Company**
www.mylifechannels.com

Library of Congress Cataloging-in-Publication Data

Printed in the United States of America.

ISBN 13: 978-0-615-23046-7
ISBN 10: 0-615-23046-6

Evangelistic work.

Editing: Mary Jones, NY

Pagination: Dominique Abney, iDesign, Carlisle, PA

Cover: Dominique Abney, iDesign, Carlisle, PA

Images: Deryl Towns, NJ

Cover Make Up: Kaseem Johnson, NJ

Inside Make Up: Atina of The Room, NJ

Hair: www.indiquehair.com

Stylist: Jummane Cain, FL

Fear is NOT My Boss is available in soft and hard cover edition

FOREWORD

When I first began to read, *Fear is Not My Boss* I literally had to pause a few times to ensure this was really written by the women I know as Ruby. And it wasn't simply because the content is so well written (because it is) or because the thoughts are congruent and flow with the literary ease of a seasoned veteran novel (because they do). No, I was given pause because the Ruby I know seems to be oblivious to the intensity of the knowledge of fear she speaks of in this book. The Ruby I know is self-confident, assertive, poised, polished and brave. Of all the attributes you could conjure up, I dare say fear would not be one of the qualities attributable to my sister.

And it is that dichotomy that draws the reader deeper into this wonderful work more so than any single element. The writing is both academic and colloquial. It is theologically sound, yet personal. It speaks of a subject most of us are all too familiar with, yet it provides insights we have missed most our lives. Let's face it; our fears (and their origin) are not something we like to talk about. But Ruby raises the disturbing, the uncomfortable and unpopular in the most calming and reassuring voice possible.

Had this book been written as a thesis by a student vying for a doctrinal degree, using essentially the same words, it would undoubtedly succeed in academia but would fail to have the total impact it has today. Had this book been written by a student seeking a degree in theology, again using many of the exact phases and concepts, it would certainly garner high praise and impressive marks, but it would not be the tool for healing and deliverance I've found it to be. The secret to the success of this blessed manuscript is the fact our author has intertwined the essence of her spirit within the pages of this project. No academic study can replace genuine experience. No theological positioning can substitute true revelation.

As much as this literary work is about the destructive nature of fear in our lives, it is also a powerful teaching tool we can use to address the many other destructive forces sent to destroy the children of Light. As I continued reading I began to understand more about the nature of all our maladies and personal battles. I believe we all will find, as Ruby obviously has, overcoming begins only when we decide to face our greatest struggles.

In closing, I pause one last time to honor God for the gift he has invested in this dear woman. The bible assures us that he has already worked out every situation in our lives for the benefit of his children. (Roman 8:28, And we know that all things work together for good to them that love God, to them who are the called according to his purpose). My victory is not mine alone, but belongs to all those that are called according to his purpose. Your pain is not yours alone, but is shared by all those called according to his purpose. Ruby testifies she was frightened. She now lives in triumph. Her triumph is not hers alone, but can now be shared by us all. We bless the Lord for this literary testimony. It will strengthen you and aid you in your time of need. It's reassuring to know, Fear is Not My Boss!

God Bless

Pastor Milton B. Hobbs

LADONAY (TO MY LORD)

You are a WONDER. I give all honor, all praise, all glory and all credit to you, from whom all blessings flow. Thank you for speaking to my spirit concerning fear and faith. Thank you for crowning me with courage to complete this work, against all odds. Thank you for granting me the inspiration and opportunity to minister life through your inspired word. In wholehearted and submissive humility, I praise you.

This companion is a written inspiration from God. I have been fortunate enough at this point and time to know Him and know His Voice. He has been with me always; He has been there when times were tough, when the winds were unpredictable, when I was afraid, when I have fallen. When I have been ridiculed, misunderstood, misrepresented. When I've been kicked and talked about. He has been with me when I've been wrong, and in sin—revealing myself to myself. He has been directly responsible, better yet solely responsible for unfolding the wrinkled possibilities and breathing life into my withering petals. He in His unwavering love has been sparing my life from dangers seen and unseen. Even when I did not deserve His favor, He blessed me. He has kept me through it all. He has led me in the path of grace and followed me with the hedge of mercy. He is an extraordinary force of love, the kind of friend I could only hope to be. God provides a path, a map, and a guiding light. He teaches us to forgive and release. Moreover, in every one of us He has imparted special gifts. He has called us to duty and will supply our every need. He never fails. What God has planned for you is for you and you alone—only your will can derail it. When we cannot realize the truth, it is because it is so hard to see in the dark.

I dedicate this inspiration especially to you, oh friend of mine!

Kindly pardon yourself from the fear that dwells in spiritual blindness and let there be light!

But now, this is what the Lord says he who created you, O Jacob, he who formed you, O Israel: "Fear not, for I have redeemed you; I have summoned you by name; you are mine. When you pass through the waters, I will be with you; and when you pass through the rivers, they will not sweep over you. When you walk through the fire, you will not be burned; the flames will not set you ablaze. For I am the Lord, your God, the Holy One of Israel, your Savior; I give Egypt for your ransom, Cush and Seba in your stead. Since you are precious and honored in my sight, and because I love you, I will give men in exchange for you, and people in exchange for your life. Do not be afraid, for I am with you; I will bring your children from the east and gather you from the west. I will say to the north, 'Give them up! And to the south, 'Do not hold them back. Bring my sons from afar and my daughters from the ends of the earth-everyone who is called by my name, whom I created for my glory, whom I formed and made." [Isaiah 43:1-7]

DEDICATION

I want to send a prayer to the heavens so that you may know you will always be precious, invaluable beyond words and a treasure unimagined. I wonder if I held your hand enough, or kissed your forehead enough, though I've kissed you a million times and more. In such a number-- my sweet and loving friend, a million kisses could never amount to the love I have burning in my heart for you. I wonder if you realize how deeply I love you, and how you are ever present in my mind. I hope you heard our heart-felt prayers at your journey's end. We, your pearls, were all there, together praying on one accord in desperate hope for your break-through. Accepting finally that God in His infinite wisdom and errorless judgment, knows best.

I thank you Mom, you have always been my friend.

ACKNOWLEGEMENTS

To my pearls, through whom I've become rich: you each are a piece of heaven! (Cecil, Sonyae, Skye, Naiani and Silva, Jules, Austi & DuJuan, Lil Vince & Scooter King, Jamar & Jasmir) I love you baby-sweets! Thank you Captain for pouring into my spirit, richness and walking with me hand in hand, heart to heart and vessel to vessel. You are a special man your gift will make room for you.

I speak to the heavens about a personal Angel, JUMA Pearl, (Julia Marie Woods-Long). She walked fearlessly and confidently in high spirit and agape love; with her, I encountered raindrops from Heaven. Juma, you were the epitome of love! I still draw from your wisdom and I will love you forever and someday meet you at the gate called Beautiful! Daddy, "Focused faith." You have so clearly mastered the power of positive thinking. No matter what the circumstance, nor how dark, all you see is light. That is faith! No matter what the odds are, all you speak is victory! That is faith. For you, winning is not the best way, it is the only way. That is endurance! All you hear is "yes." Daddy, not only is that faith, that is beautiful. Robyn, Alton, James, Jamey and Anthony—you too are pearls…I am so blessed to be in the middle of treasured of gems. I am further blessed by the wonderful soulmates God sent to you, with whom you have become one: Richard, Tracey, Sharice and Schneider. To my Uncles who have found Christ where He has always been, inside! To my aunts, Molly, Ruby, Mary and Auntie Jo my nearest and dearest. To Nana, Elder Isabelle Long, for praying without ceasing. Pastor Elsa DeSouza a selfless and unfailing friend who walks in the love and the grace of God. Shammah Womack, thank you for touching my brokenness and demanding that I stand. Evangelist Myla Giles, for the power of worship. Adrienne Brand for demanding that I stand! To Voni, my soldier. Chi my connected one! God is going to use you in a mighty tender way, Tiny Woman of Great Faith. Tauheedah for teaching me to seek. Judea Freeman (Gerry & Lolita), you made me thirst for more…Rhoda Phillips Daniels (S Munn Ruby) who I knew for a short season as a child-- where ever you are and your parents, thank you for taking me to church, it was then that God truly touched me and saved my soul. Rev. Milton Hobbs Jr. you are a wonderful, friend, Pastor and teacher, a gift from on high! You will never know how instrumental you have been in the scheme of things, but God knows. Love you so dearly! There have been countless others: LaWanda, DuJour, Marcia, Victory, Theresa, Merri, Stacy, Lisa, Lillian, Tracey, Ane, Debbie, Michelle, Stella, Shawna. To God's wonders; Dr. Walcott, Dr. Kevin Holder, Nassar Ameen, The late Dr. Donald Womack and Bishop Milton Hobbs Senior, two of the most amazing spiritual fathers. To Bishop, Aaron Hobbs, and 1st Lady Valerie Hobbs for the love! Pastor Yvette Anderson, you are a rare jewel. Pastor Derrick Greene, God makes all things beautiful in His time. What a plentiful gift in you. Pastor Paul and Sharon Dean, for praying tender heartedly. "aiM" for your ministry of "helps," thanks for the torch! To Minister Gwendolyn Battle, Gods tenacious prayer warrior... To my husband, Cecil (Q, Captain) you said something very profound to me. You ministered to my spirit when I was discouraged by my many attempts to complete my projects in the past. You said "Honey, this is not your first book, you have been writing, for years and years. This book is merely the fine print of what has always been released.

His words; "reflections of the words were written before and can be found in the hearts and paths of the many people that you have poured into over the years." I'd never thought of it that way. I saw the half-full glass as half-empty. If I can be frank, I wondered when I could ever finish. This book has been my mind's companion for so many years...the fact that it is in your hands today, that is my testimony! We as more than hearers, but doers, have to look up and beyond rather than behind and down. If you have, like I have, in times past been guilty of procrastination and have derailed dreams here and there, don't allow those bumps in the road to define where you are going. Adopt the position that says "so what" to the past incompletes. No matter what they may be, from this point on take it by force and prevail! And by all means, FEAR NOT! A special thank you to April Gregory, of AG Consulting for inspiring me. You were the obedient voice that spoke to me at the appointed hour and I thank you.

I pray that God covers my spiritual contributors. You are all awesome in your own right. I am happy to have traveled and journeyed with you in the things of God. May the grace, presence, mercy and favor of God rest upon you and yours as you delight yourself in Him!

TABLE OF CONTENTS

PREFACE

WE OUGHT TO BE HIGH ACHIEVERS, OH YES! WHY?
SIMPLY BECAUSE WE AS CHILDREN OF THE GOSPEL ARE
CALLED TO GREATNESS. I SAY IN WISDOM, WHATEVER
YOU STAND FOR, BACK IT UP WITH FAITH.

There are varying avenues to higher ground. But I dare you to couple God's plan for you with your perceived purpose in life by practicing the art of prayer in sincere faith. In prayer you will explore an intimate walk and discover a sacred peace that surpasses all understanding. Know that no matter the issue, God provides a way of escape and salvation through Him. The Lord is good!

As I go forth in my discussion of fear and its potential to overtake us, I pray that you will become cognizant enough to recognize and identify the evidence of **operation fear.** It's a sly spirit that has a major goal: to rule over you. In life we develop fear that the adversary uses against us. We also use fear against ourselves and others. Either way, fear is not a part of God's plan. There are things that are predicated upon the spirit of fear by design. Once you become sensitive in spirit, you will recognize these designs by the fruit bared.

HOW TO WEATHER THE STORM

The adversary will use "fear" and the "fear of" to manipulate and control you. One area for example is by planting deceitful seeds of prosperity. Let us be perfectly clear: the adversary does not fight fair. It is his orchestrated wish that we underachieve in spirit and in truth. He does this to distract us and distort our natural sight by keeping our focus on material gain. Friends, do not get caught up majoring in the minors in life. The Prince of Darkness wants to make racing rats out of us by magnifying the pleasures of the flesh. He does this so that we are too occupied chasing the dreams of this world to experience the true fruits of the spirit. But the word of God says that a true soldier does not entangle himself in the affairs of this life. What the world offers is fallen fruit, but God offers fruit that brings life. One of our greatest problems today is the overwhelming emphasis on teaching prosperity in the form of material gain. While the favor of God grants such blessings, there is a greater urgency for Godly prosperity and richness of spirit. It is dangerous to look to the blessing when praising, rather than the source of these blessings. It is not the blessing that will keep us prosperous, it is God—our lifeline. "For the time will come when they will not endure sound doctrine, but according to their own desires, because they have itching ears, they will heap up for themselves teachers, and they will turn their ears away from the truth and be turned aside to fables." [2 Timothy 4:3]

For there will come a time when they will not endure sound doctrine. But according to their own desires, because they have itching ears they will heap up for themselves teachers. And they will turn their ears away from the truth and be turned aside to fables.

That time is now. People are turning away from the truth, the lifeline. People are caught up in the cares of this world, not concerned with their souls. These individuals hear what they want to hear, about houses with massive closet space, cars, and money. Following only those who talk their talk and walk their walk. We are so caught up in the fascinations of the world that we are willing to be fed soothe-saying myths instead of sound doctrine. In this life we equate "making it" with material gain, status, and acceptance. When we don't have it, we "gotta" get it. When we get it, it's never enough, and so the ambiance dissipates. You must consider what's the good life, for you?

Jot down your idea of a good life on the next page.

_____

_____

_____

_____

_____

_____

_____

_____

_____

_____

_____

_____

_____

_____

_____

Once you have finished this book, return to what you've written. I guarantee you will revise it. God Himself wants a truly good life for all of us. He makes all things possible, if you only believe.

God wants to bless us through our faith, works, obedience, honor, submission and love; not necessarily in and of our own efforts (i.e. accomplishments, scorecard, or status). Be smart enough to know that it is His hand alone that keeps us.

> *Otherwise you may say in your hearts, "my power and the strength of my hands have produced this wealth for me.* [Deuteronomy 8:17]

> *For you, brothers, were called to freedom. Only do not turn your freedom into an opportunity to gratify your flesh, but through love make it your habit to serve one another* [Galatians 5:13]

> *Both riches and honor come from You, (God) and You rule over all, and in Your hand is power and might; and it lies in Your hand to make great and to strengthen everyone.* [1 Chronicles 29:12]

God's strength is made perfect in your weakness, but you must surrender and serve Him to activate this truth. If we allow the mountains and valleys in our lives to become the God we serve, we are planting seeds of death mentally, physically and spiritually. Don't allow "things" (material gain or the lack thereof) to become what defines you, what promotes or demotes your motivation. It will drive you to your wits end and become the possessing power that determines your outcome. *Now may the Lord of peace give you His peace at all times and in every way.* [2 Thessalonians 3:16]

"I know fear—a companion no more." It is my prayer that you will enjoy the peace of knowing, understanding, and believing that the battle does not have to be yours: you can simply step aside and, in faith, give it to God. You can become content in knowing that you are covered in the perfection of His love. I know it can be difficult, but it does become easier over time. Seek! That's all— simply seek! You will find shelter in the storm. "All things work together for good to them that love the Lord; and to them that are called according to His purpose." [Romans 8:28].

It is a shame to know that some people will literally take their lives when they fear the loss of what they considered "gain." There is something terribly wrong with equating the "gift of life" to the "things in life" we acquire. If your faith is in failure, by faith you fail. However if your faith is in the promises, the promises will birth blessings. It is all according to your faith. Don't meditate on the negative, by doing so you bring life to pondered doom. Instead meditate on that which is good and pure; inherit the miracles and wonders that were predestined for you. The bottom line is that God absolutely loves you. In fact, he adores you.

> *Many are the afflictions of the righteous but God delivers us from them all.* [Psalm 34:19]

God's hand is always there, guiding and protecting. When I give Him the praise, the honor, and the glory—both now and forever more—it is because all the glory belongs to Him and Him alone!

Cleanliness is next to Godliness, you've heard this time and time again. He is not just talking about your surroundings; he is speaking about a clean heart. Make a decision to clean up your act and assume your righteous position. In order for us to win the battle that is before us, we need to stand clean before God, repenting daily and going before His throne. Where is the throne? It's right here, right now. It is where you can inhale the essence of Jesus and acquire eternal light. It is in knowing that you need Him and you need Him now.

We are enslaved in the maintenance of our images. When one door shuts, another door opens. Did you not get the memo? Fear, especially the spirit of fear, is conniving. It distracts us from what really matters in life. I hope to help you so you may distinguish between the "gift of life" and the "gifts in life."

Place Your Hand on Your Heart and Pray with Me...

Ask the Lord to open your spiritual eyes in that you may soar as an eagle.

Ask God to deliver you from fear, doubt, judgement, and unforgiveness.

It is time to forgive others and it is time to forgive yourself

Psalm 91:

He who dwells in the shelter of the Most High will rest in the shadow of the Almighty. I will say of the Lord, "He is my refuge and my fortress, my God, in whom I trust." Surely he will save you from the fowler's snare and from the deadly pestilence. He will cover you with his feathers, and under his wings you will find refuge; his faithfulness will be your shield and rampart. You will not fear the terror of night, nor the arrow that flies by day, nor the pestilence that stalks in the darkness, nor the plague that destroys at midday. A thousand may fall at your side, ten thousand at your right hand, but it will not come near you. You will only observe with your eyes and see the punishment of the wicked. If you make the Most High your dwelling— even the Lord, who is my refuge- then no harm will befall you no disaster will come near your tent. For he will command his angels concerning you to guard you in all your ways; they will lift you up in their hands, so that you will not strike your foot against a stone. You will tread upon the lion and the cobra; you will trample the great lion and the serpent. "Because he loves me," says the Lord, "I will rescue him; I will protect him, for he acknowledges my name. He will call upon me, and I will answer him; I will be with him in trouble, I will deliver him and honor him. With long life will I satisfy him and show him my salvation."

PART I:

Weather the Storm

CHAPTER 1

Tidal Waves

In the tidal waves of my life, I was blessed enough to witness the power of the true and living God, who calmed the storms that surrounded me. While the story behind my tidal waves is short, the message is grand. God really doesn't want us to suffer from our mistakes. He imparts His word to give us clues and clear direction. Even as a very young child I was able to see that we should not take matters into our own hands without seeking God the Father for direction. When we do, the outcome is usually not favorable. When we take matters into our own hands we tend to get in the way of what God has planned for us. When we give our battles over to God we can be confident in a victorious outcome, as God can do anything but fail.

Most of my relatives call me Ruby. I was named after my Great Aunt Ruby Jane Pierson who lived close by. I was raised in a house near a corner lot that housed a garage and a huge pear tree, with branches full of low-hanging fruit. I recall my older siblings would climb this tree to recline on the roof of the garage. After playing, we would often return home by passing near our neighbor's fence. This was frequently an intimidating experience. Our next-door neighbor had a malicious dog that seemed to go ballistic at the sight of us. Kahsei was a Siberian Husk whom we often referred to as "the demon dog." He would bark, growl, snarl, foam at the mouth and bang viciously against the fence. It was as if he was trying to tear it down, and indeed, after a time he knocked a couple of the wooden planks off of the fence, so his rage became visual.

Sometimes Kahsei would break free and come running after us; we would be so frightened we would climb the pear tree to get on the garage roof until he was captured. I was afraid of heights, but I was more afraid of that dog. The adrenaline rush allowed me to climb that tree in record time, finding safety on the garage.

On one particular day this dog managed to break loose and attack my baby brother, sinking his teeth into his little hand. My brother had to have reconstructive surgery to put his hand back together. We began to live in constant fear as the dog continued to torment us day after day. We tried to make ourselves safe. We deliberately kept bats and bricks all over the back yard for protection.

The reality of this very real threat to his family's safety infuriated my Father, so he decided to take matters into his own hands. I remember my Dad preparing raw ground beef laced with broken glass and rat poison. He pushed it through the open fence and watched Kahasei devour this deadly meal. We waited anxiously to see what would happen. Nothing. For days, nothing. That dog never got sick, he didn't die, and he was not harmed in any way. We remained too afraid to play near the fence.

Soon after this incident with the dog my Nanna arrived from North Carolina. She was the sort of woman who flew up to pray with us whenever any of our family had the smallest crisis. Nanna was a prayer warrior and a woman of great faith. She would pray in faith and God delivered time after time. When Nanna arrived in New Jersey she began to pray, anointing the house and everyone in it. A few days after the blessing, Kahasei broke his chain and killed a neighbor's poodle, resulting in a court order to have Kahasei put to sleep. Everything was alright. In retrospect, I can only wonder how much terror could have been avoided had we placed Faith over Fear!

If you are toiling with something in your life and the burden of your storm seems greater than you, it is probably high time that you get out of the way and allow God to do what He does best. Give the battle to God and begin to operate in the faith and assurance that He is Lord. In the meantime ride it out.

I am pleased that you have decided to examine this spiritual companion and inspiration. It is my intent that you set yourself free to soar, as endless possibilities unfold before you. You are a Kingdom child and have been fearlessly fashioned for greatness both now and forever more. Yes, set yourself free by escaping the boundaries of your own desires and leaping onward to the unlimited promises that God has absolutely etched for you. Why go through life shackled by your own means, when you can walk through open doors that lead to abundant living. God wants more for you than you could ever imagine for yourself.

This memoir opens past doors and shared experiences in order to express how God molded and developed my character. You may have similar stories that you have gone through at some point and time that perhaps you can draw from to gain insightful knowledge around its purpose. God is a revealer! So please, bare with me as I attempt to lead you through the corridors of my storms. I pray that this helps you to understand your purpose and the importance of protecting your purpose. I pray also that you adopt the urgency to trust God and to obey Him. Finally, it is my prayer that the peace of God, be with you.

CHAPTER 2

Undercurrents

As children, we see and experience so many things that plant seeds in our lives. These deposits contribute tremendously to our growth process. Some of these seed deposits are responsible for our strengths and virtues; others are accountable for areas of weakness, error, and trouble. To right ourselves we often have to trace back to the source and erase it through personal rebuke and affirmation in God. It may require hard work, persistence, and diligence, but freedom of fear is worth every ounce of the hard work required to achieve living joy as it pertains to your life. I pray that God opens your understanding of self—as he has done for me—and ushers in a sense of freedom that allows you to escape the walls that stand between you and your potential.

From the time I first laid eyes on my brother James, I found him absolutely beautiful. I felt James was one of the most gorgeous babies anyone could ever imagine. He was round with large, joy-filled eyes, cute dimples and long curly hair, beautiful caramel skin...Everyone loved him. As he grew, it was clear that he was highly favored by God himself.

My grandparents lived a few minutes away from us in a smart, modern-style house with a huge built-in pool. We spent most of our summer days there, and so we were all comfortable with water and learned to swim well. Even at only two or three years-old, my brother was so brave; I'd taken to calling him "Fearless James." As a toddler, he would plead with us to go "wimmin'." He would run towards that pool every chance he got. I remember my Mom screaming because she couldn't swim, and couldn't jump in after him. I watched James sink down as bubbles came up, his pretty eyes looking up through the water in excitement and glee. It was strange, realizing this little baby didn't understand the danger he was in. He actually seemed to enjoy it. I realize now that babies don't recognize fear: they have innate faith.

My Dad jumped in and saved Fearless James. To his delight, he discovered that James had been blowing out of his nose the entire time—he somehow knew not to breathe under water. James continued to jump into water whenever he could—by the age of 4, he was swimming like a fish. I on the other hand slipped into the deep end of the pool before I learned to swim, and nearly drowned. I had to have my stomach pumped. This scared the daylight out of me, and though I later learned to swim, the scar remained, and I always respected the water.

We have all experienced things or events from the past that have an impact on how we ultimately handle things: whether in a negative manner or a positive perspective. We are shaped genetically, environmentally, socially and spiritually. As parents we should go over and beyond to teach our children to listen to the Spirit, to teach them who they are in God so that they can handle life's challenges with balance and clarity. As I recall some of my experiences and how they magnified my fears, I really believe that I had the power all along to address these inhibitions. Through seeking, finding, learning, and applying I became stronger spiritually; everything else lined up. I am sure you can do the same. If you can recall and identify the source of your fears, you can address them and move on.

For a long time, even as an adult, I slept with a night-light. As a child I was afraid to go to the bathroom in the dark, so I wet the bed if I thought I saw a shadow or something. It was probably a robe hanging on the door. But I was immobilized with fear, so much that I'd lay there and stress my bladder and urinary tract. I can attribute one act of innocence in the name of fun that exacerbated my fear. My older brother and sister used to set up our basement like a haunted cellar. They would gather all the baby dolls and stuffed animals in the house, smearing oatmeal around the mouths as vomit, ketchup in their eyes to simulate blood. Then they would lock me in the basement. I was seven years old or so and this was just the beginning of seeded fear. It was purposed in fun, but I sat stiff with terror as they would flick the lights on and off, making haunting noises through the door. To this day the sight of blood makes me weak.

CHAPTER 3

Wind Driven

Too frequently I heard my mother screaming and pleading for help. She was a battered wife in love with an unfaithful man who offered her only a fraction of his heart. Marriage is work, yet too many want to show up late, punch out early, or work on outside projects. They forget about the bond of marriage and the mate whom they promised to love and honor. The commitment, in and of itself, is a promise to keep your word before the Father in the presence of witnesses. Too many people take marriage far too lightly. When I look back on my first experience, witnessing marriage, as I knew it from my eyes as a child, I can honestly say that what I experienced was not the best example of honor and obedience. Even love, for that matter. One day I woke up to change. It seemed as though a breeze came through to gently tug on the spirit of my loved ones. Each change took place at an unpredictable time, and by the time it was over I was released from the fear of some terrible event.

My Dad, though somewhat a different man today, was a true southern disciplinarian. *"Spare the rod, spoil the Child."* He loved us, provided for us, protected us, but make no mistakes he delivered his wrath whenever he deemed it necessary. Now, I was the kind of child who would not take a spanking easily. I was fast, agile, and fearful. He had to chase me around the house, pulling me from under tables and beds, out of closets, often too winded to deliver punishment. After he had rested, however, he would catch me later off guard. Daddy would make us pick out our own "appropriate switch," and it had to be a good one. He would pull off one leaf at a time, asking us to rehash our misbehavior and explain just what we had done wrong. This tormenting conversation was somewhat antagonistic, using fear as the foundation. Dad said it was important for kids to understand exactly what they did wrong so that they would not repeat the same bad behaviors.

One time Dad told me to go and take a bath and then he pulled me out of the tub by one arm and spanked me wet. I vowed to never treat my children the way that I was treated. My children don't know anything about punishment like I knew it.

One Christmas morning, I was sitting on my mother's lap, kissing her and thanking her for my wonderful gifts. My Dad walked over and demanded I get up, clearly very upset. My Mom pulled me close saying, "She's just fine, she can stay." Enraged, he grabbed my arm and jerked me from her lap. He told her to come upstairs now. When she got to the top of the stairs, I heard her scream, then the sound of her body as she tumbled down the steps. I ran to her. She had a black eye; the other eye was swollen with tears. Seconds later, the doorbell rang: it was her brother Jimmy with our Christmas gifts. Seeing his sobbing sister's face, Uncle Jim grabbed my Dad and started slapping him back and forth. My Mom screamed, "Don't hurt him, Jim!" so my uncle got upset and left.

This was just one of many days gone wrong on High Street. As a child I thought it was my fault because I was on her lap, though in later years I learned that it had absolutely nothing to do with me, but something to do with one of his affairs. My parents' frequent fights caused me to dread losing my Mother. When my parents would get all dressed up to go to events, I was afraid something might go wrong, and she would never come back.

My bedroom window overlooked the side street that led to our driveway. I would lie in bed and cry until they returned, because I did not trust my Father. Every time a car would go by, I would run to the window, eager to see Mom's safe arrival. I don't think anyone knew that I lived in this manner, overcome by thoughts that I would lose my Mother.

I was about eleven years old when the huge truck pulled in. Mom decided to move us to what she called a "spacious luxury apartment." Having always grown up in houses, my Mom was always interested in high-rise apartment style living. It tickled her fancy: the idea of a doorman, a garbage shoot. She loved the place, and so did I. After the truck was packed, it was time to drive over to the apartment in a separate car. Dad came out and clapped his hands.

"Let's go," he commanded.

Mom looked at him boldly. "You are not coming with us."

As she got into her car, she gripped the wheel and fell apart. I was proud of her, but I hurt for her, and for him. It took great courage and strength of mind to walk away from a 16-year marriage to a man she completely adored. She faced her fear and handled the business at hand. In a way, he met his fear, and managed to overcome it.

In retrospect, I don't think my mom left him because she feared what he would do to her. I think she left him, because she feared missing out on love; she had endured to the end, and couldn't take anymore. My Mom was famous for saying "When you are full, you'll push the plate away." I understand this better with each passing day. You can never tell what motivates a person to change the scene, but it is important that they do in fact change it.

Mom's "Honey" came into her life a few years later, restoring her joy and smile. Grantley was a wonderful, kind man, and their relationship was mutually uplifting. While I am sorry my parents split up, if they had not, I would never have seen the glow my Mother had upon finding friendship and love all at once.

In 1981, my baby sister was born. I was right there. I was there to see my Mother handle pain with courage and strength. It was such a beautiful and enlightening experience. Giving birth is much like overcoming fear, you know? It requires a warrior's spirit....you see it, you prepare for it, you focus on breathing, and you fight.

If fear is the ever-present energy in which we are submerged, we become fear advocates, bullied by time and space. Fear is dynamic when we allow it to occupy our time. It stands between you and your purpose, you and your victory, you and your joy, me and everything that is great and promised to me. Who did you love that if only you had....What did you miss if only you had....When did you stop if only you had finished... Why continue along this venture of being separated from your purpose and what you are entitled to in this lifetime, simply because fear shaped your decision? Fear can creep into your home, your career, your relationships and your goals. Why don't you go further in your education? If we really look at the reason, fear is hiding some where in the foundation of the why-not's. Have you been at the same level in your career for a great length of time? What's stopping you from accelerating the professional you? What is in the way of elevating the Holy Spirit that dwells in you? Who says you won't make it if you change directions, or if you stand alone, or stand united for all the right reasons?

You never really walk alone anyway. The mighty God we serve has never really left you in the dry land. Remember that there is value in the valley, wisdom in the wilderness, safety in the midst of the storm, a wheel in the middle of the wheel, a ram in the bush, a testimony out of every test and a very mighty God on our side.

Life without lessons makes you susceptible to immoral conduct, sinful thinking, errors, and redundant mistakes. My friend Angie always says, "Catch it. Learn it." Notice that after the storm, you're still standing. Seriously assess the settling of the dust: you've made it through. Why not address the important factors in your life today, right here, and right now! What are we waiting for anyway? What could bring greater joy than discovering and living out your purpose?

"Faith without works is dead, just as the body without spirit is lifeless." [James 2:26] If something is going to change for the better, you have to step out on faith to activate your potential. God will take two steps for every one you take; He will see you through. We as believers and doers of the word cannot simply sit around twiddling our fingers until something happens. We have to move. Water without movement will develop a film of bacterial foam. Eventually that growth, nurtured from stagnation, will begin to take on the aroma of rot and death. The vitality of the water is gone—it becomes useless and dangerous to ingest. Yet water that flows stays fresh and clean. It has life and preserves life. Imagine if our inner fluids ceased to flow, we would surely deteriorate and surely die. In the same spirit, neither your dreams nor your purpose will be made manifest if you remain stagnate. You must put your desires into operation. Get up! Get up and do what you were meant to do! Don't lie still until you begin to stink—get moving, live a faith-filled life of activity! God has created you and equipped you with everything it takes to march in victory.

CHAPTER 4

Cyclone

God is real and true, and His mercy endures forever. I was nineteen on this night of hell. My cyclone experience shares a nightmare that drastically crippled my ability to know joy and to experience peace on my own. When and if a day such as this day should come, you should know that God and only God can heal you, lift you up and carry you through such a storm. Prayer is the only answer. Had it not been for Him, I am not sure that I could have held myself together emotionally. We—that is, all affected by this event—were covered by God's grace. He delicately housed our emotions, broken spirits, our hours of devastation.

You may have experienced a cyclone, but you should know that God will restore all the wind has stolen. You will breathe normally again, your heart will return to its natural rhythm, the sun will shine on your face and the tears will find their place. You will get back up again and you will learn to rest in serenity. You will be healed, delivered, set free. And as to our loved ones, you will release the flower of their souls to God's garden, where they will grow forever, never to be plucked again.

For a teenager, a part-time job builds character, establishes a sense of responsibility, and exercises financial freedom. But equally important a lesson is selecting the right job—allowing your parents or loved ones to be involved in the process helps, too. This way those who care for you can assess what is best for you to hopefully weed out opportunities that may not be the best option for you. When I rushed into things, my mother would say to me, "You just had to be so fast, that's your problem."

She wanted me to really look at my associations to ascertain if they would be fruitful; if not, she would redirect my path. I was the kid that always wanted to work. Initially it was to buy Christmas gifts for my siblings, then it was for personal spending. As a single and struggling parent, my Mom did not have the finances to pay for anything other than the necessities. My first job was at the age of ten: I would sweep the outside of a store on Orange Road. Later, I would shovel snow in the neighborhood. During summer months I even sold lemonade and mud pies. Yes real mud pies, bless the tender-hearted adults who supported my little business.

I always had an enterprising mind. By the time I turned four-teen I was able to work through a program called Summer Youth Employment designed to employ youth over the summer months. This was the perfect plan to finance my school wardrobe, but when school started I needed money to get by. So my buddies and I decided to take a part-time job working for Mr. Howard. He had a daughter and a son that attended our high school as well. Mr. Howard paid fifty cents more than minimum wage, so we seized the opportunity. He had several corporate cleaning accounts in the area; all we had to do was meet him at his house, where he would carpool us in his spotless van to his accounts. Mr. Howard was passionate about his van. At first we thought he was joking about docking us for breaking "van rules," but when the check came, it was real.

He had so many rules that by the time you got compensated for you work, your check would be reduced ridiculously because of deductions, for conduct and imperfect performance. If you hypothetically earned $110 for the week, he would have an itemized list of deductions that reduced your check to $28. He would deduct for a streak on the bathroom mirror, finger-prints on his van windows, if you slammed the van door, if the garbage bags were not tied properly, if you laughed too much. It was unbareable.

Watch out for unreasoning spirits. It is a clear tale-tale sign that the end result will not be peaceful.

My younger brother decided that he wanted to make money too, so I had a talk with Mr. Howard and he hired my younger brother. The first day of work, my brother James got into the van and apparently he shut the van door too hard. Mr. Howard was so perturbed he pulled a knife on James, vowing not to pay him for the week. James was so upset that he told my mother. Livid, my Mother stormed over to Mr. Howard's home to reason with him. He refused to hear my mother—he refused to consider her views, or anyone's for that matter. I still remember my mother's firm instruction on that day: "That man ain't right—he is sadistic and hateful and he's not balanced. Leave him, his van and his job alone—it ain't worth it." I eavesdropped on her phone conversation with my great aunts, discussing

Mr. Howard's demeanor, how his eyes didn't look right. Following our mother's direction, we resigned.

I had other jobs in high school: I worked for Burger King, then Bradlee's department store, followed by Marshall's outlet. Finally during my senior year, I landed an office position just a few blocks away from the high school. My friends Terri and Theresa (identical twins) continued to work for Mr. Howard for quite some time. Our varying schedules did not allow us to see each other as much as we used to but we managed here and there. Theresa was appointed office manager handling the books and payroll, though she quit after Mr. Howard began flirting with her.

Terri was then promoted to Theresa's old position. Learning such office skills in high school was an impressive accomplishment. I thought that was a good opportunity at the time; in fact, we all did. I remember thinking to myself, *if Mom hadn't forced me to quit, I could have learned as well.* But just like God knows what is best, mothers usually have a pretty good idea as well.

After high school I left for college, and Terri and Theresa went to ABI Business Institute. We would catch up as often as we could. I saw Theresa more than Terri because Terri also worked full time in addition to attending business school. She was focused and doing so well. Theresa transferred to Bloomfield College, where she later earned a degree in Finance, the same degree Terri was perusing at ABI. We were all good kids transitioning to young adults, all of us in pursuit of bright futures.

It was the summer of 1986, August 9th when my older brother Alton threw a back-to-school party. It was purposed to be a joyful sending off celebration for a football scholar returning to school. Alton hosted the party in my grandparent's back yard: a spacious pool, a big back yard, a patio large enough for dancing, and a barbeque area made it the perfect location. The summer had come to an end for us college students, so August 9th was the last day to jam. Carlos (Terri and Theresa's brother) was in charge of the DJ booth, spinning our favorite summer dance songs: "Body to Body," "Set It Off," Adeva's "Respect" and Charvoni's "Always There." We all loved music and we loved to dance. The yard was crowded with Montclair High School graduates, family and friends. Even some parents and grand parents cut a little rug that night.

While everyone felt something in the air, no one anticipated the travesty that was soon to come. At some point during the party, I left to call my boyfriend at that time. My grandmother kept her phone locked up in her bedroom whenever there were parties to keep the kids from running up the phone bill.

I went to Terri and Theresa's house through the front door; Terri showed up within minutes, having learned that I had gone up the street to use her phone. Her behavior was strange and she just kept rushing me. While I was talking with my boyfriend, the operator interrupted, requesting an emergency break-through call from Clarissa Howard, Mr. Howard's daughter.

"No Rube, don't accept the call," Terri pleaded. But Clarissa kept calling, trying to get through. When I hung up the phone, it immediately rang. It was a local funeral home.

"I understand there is a body to be picked up," the stranger on the other end told us. Terri and I were terribly confused: no one had called for a pick up, and there was no dead body.

"You must have the wrong number," I said.

"Is this 335 Orange Road?" He asked.

"Yes"

"Oh…Sorry for the inconvenience."

Then Terri and Theresa's grandmother—whom they affectionately called Mother—overheard us. She shared a story about the night prior, when she and Theresa saw what they thought was a body dressed in white laying on Orange Road. Mother said they had called the police, but when the police arrived there was no body at all. Mother was getting up there in age, but Theresa was only nineteen, so this was something more than the mind playing tricks.

The story seemed to make Terri more nervous. She seemed rushed, saying over and over, "Let's go, let's get back to the party." I proceeded toward the front door, but Terri directed me through the kitchen, down the back steps, through the basement, and out the cellar door. It was like an obstacle course, leaving this way, but she insisted and led me all the way by my hand.

Once outside, Terri instructed me to go ahead—she had forgotten something inside, and would meet up with me at the party. This was all so odd; I could feel that something wasn't right. But I let Terri go back inside, then out the front door in the opposite direction while I went the other way. Once I returned to the party, I felt afraid, but I did not know why.

As I reflect on that party, I think of how Terri insisted that Theresa and I taste her food. We all had the same food on our plates, but she insisted that hers tasted special. It was as if Terri hung on to every spice, savoring the flavor intensely. So we complied by eating her food and sipping her beverage. Terri smiled as she made us agree that her stuff was the best. Theresa's countenance was suddenly unsettling. Her emotional state was torn between anger and disbelief; she was clearly unhappy, barely concealing her emotions. Terri had somewhat of a nonchalant expression on her face, while Theresa looked as though she was beyond tears. The three of us were so close we could discern each other's emotions. After eating we went into the bathroom all at once to fix our hair, makeup, and clothes. I remember how Terri looked in the mirror while fixing her hair; gazing so intensely it looked as if she was piercing into her very own soul.

Something about the way the twins looked, coupled with the emergency break through attempts and the "wrong number" upset me. I went to my older brother Alton—he was the "football star" who, at the time, I thought could save the world. I grabbed his hand.

"Something is going on," I whispered

"What's going on?" he asked, concerned.

"I don't know, but it's real bad. I think something is happening."

I guess because of my sketchy details, he didn't believe me—he brushed me off. It was a few moments later that Mr. Howard came into the party. He stood coldly, glaring at Terri. Then he made a gesture to her, and Terri jumped to her feet. She climbed into that perfect van, and he drove her away immediately. Everyone who saw him at the party remembers him looking sadistic, sick—like some evil control freak. We all felt a sense of uneasiness. The DJ stopped the record for no reason, Theresa was suddenly crying. When the music stopped we heard gunshots. At that point the DJ, Terri and Theresa's brother, told everyone to go home. "The party is over."

Days later, I learned that Terri had escaped from being locked up in one of Mr. Howard's apartments. He had forbidden her to leave, but Theresa somehow smuggled her out so she could join us at the pool party. Had I known, had we known, maybe things would have ended differently. God has given us intuitive power called discernment. So many of us felt the presence of danger that night, yet we did not understand it. It is so important to get connected and stay connected. You just never know.

Just minutes before midnight on August 9th, 1986, Terri was gunned down in front of her home. Mr. Howard drove her away from the party, parking directly in front of her home. He opened the door for her to exit his van; when she began to run towards the safety of her home, he whipped the car around, cutting her off. Then he jumped out and opened fire. Our good friend Kim who lived next door happened to be looking out of his front window and witnessed the screeching halt of the van and the brutal murder. He shot her twenty one times. Could you imagine? She was not even twenty years old. He unloaded, reloaded, and unloaded again. He shot Terri—a baby girl, just a teenager, just out of high school, someone's daughter. He shot her in her face first, then her hands, torso, legs, back. He opened fire on this defenseless child like she was a target at a shooting range.

This was the most traumatic event of my life. I literally, along with her family, friends and bystanders, watched her life-force slip away. It took years to release the recurring visions of this night from my mind, my body, and my spirit. The truth is this pain was deeply locked within the fibers of my everything.

I will never forget how I felt driving up Granada Place towards the twin's house. I got out of the car holding my face, somehow knowing that Terri had been shot. I knew Mr. Howard had done it. There were so many people out there crowding around screaming and crying and watching in shock. Terri was in the middle of the street. Her older brother John could not bare to see his sister lying there, in the middle of the street like that. He tried to pick her up to move her closer to the side walk. The sound of her voice tore my soul apart as she cried out, "No, no, no, it hurts."

The paramedics arrived. Theresa was screaming as she ran, trying to get to her twin, but the paramedics intervened, holding her back so that they could tend to Terri. It was too much for me to process. I started backing up towards my car. I could barely control my physical body as I drove in the direction of my home. I ran through every stop sign and red light because I was trembling so uncontrollably. When I got in front of my house—and honestly, I don't know how I got there—I threw the gear into park, without stopping the car. I managed to get to the front door, but the keys were in the ignition, my car still running in the middle of Glenridge Avenue with the door open. I ran to my front door, banging and screaming to get in. My sister ran to open the door; she later said it sounded as if I were being attacked, pleading for my life. Once inside, I went straight to the bathroom and jumped in an empty bathtub. My sister tried to ask me what was wrong. I screamed out "Terry is dead" but she thought I was delusional. I lay there still, refusing to come out. In complete shock, I stayed there until my Mom came home and coaxed me out.

My Mother called Mountainside Hospital to confirm what happened. A part of me was stripped and torn to ashes, if you can imagine that. Earlier that evening we were together at a pool party, having fun. Then the ambulance arrived and she was crying out "It hurts… no—no…it hurts." You can't begin to imagine how painful this was for every one of us. Terri was so strong. I can't believe how she was able to even murmur a word at this point, but she did.

For me, the trauma of this horror resulted in a mountain of fear, anxiety, phobia, panic, discontent, hurt, anger, and pure pain. This kind of emotional baggage stays with you. Now, I despise guns, obsessive behaviors, controlling personalities, controlling spirits, violent acts and so on. I remember this mans personality and his ways, and I held that in a mental box. I boxed those scenes and packed them away somewhere deep within. I as an adult have worked through serious trust issues concerning the capabilities of others.

It was so odd how Terri wanted us to taste her food, taste her cake and taste her beverage. We all had our own of the same food but she insisted that we eat from her plate. Did Terri know that this would be her last supper—our last meal together? Did she know? That evening she was wearing all white, like the vision Theresa and Mother had the night before Terri's murder. To this very day, I remember everything Terri said and did on the night of her death. I have even stored the last time she smiled in my memories.

Although it is vague, I think it was either Stuart or Kim that called my parents to tell them that Mr. Howard was at large. Howard had called the local police department, admitting to the crime. He vowed to turn himself in after he finished off those closest to Terri: Theresa her twin, Ruby her best friend, Scooter her first love, and Kim her friend and neighbor. He was truly a sick man, just like my Mom said he was. I once heard Maya Angelou say, "When people show you who they are, believe them." This makes perfect sense to me. This man was not balanced, and we took that for granted. No one knows what we should have done or how we should have acted. It's just so hard to accept what happened.

He was apprehended just before the burial. They called the officers on duty at the funeral to let us know that they had him. We were under twenty-four-hour police protection in our homes, because of his sick threats. He made several attempts to hurt us, each time he got away. They finally found him in one of his cleaning contract's warehouse, trembling in a corner, weak and timid. In his van, the police found several weapons with enough rounds to wipe out a crowd of people.

By May or June of 1987 I had to go to trial to identify him. I was shocked to see this former clean-shaven man with a full bared and significant weight gain. Even though his look changed, the evil that he possessed remained. He looked at me with the eyes of Satan: cold, hard and threatening. I was shaken up seeing him, knowing what he was capable of. I heard Mr. Howard died of natural causes, two years into serving his sentence. Truthfully, I was relieved. It ended my taunting and recurring nightmares about him coming after me.

Terri was absolutely beautiful inside and out. She had a smile that would captivate anyone. She was a true sweet heart. Terri danced with her shoulders low but always with a joy-filled smile as she popped her fingers to the beat, waving her arm in a circular motion. She and

Theresa, they were awesome to be around—awe inspiring. Everyone loved them. I keep returning to Terri's last supper in my mind. She looked beyond herself and remained brave. Terri went to heaven. Terri Lucille Walker, an Angel in Glory, I know. In tragedies like this, there is no five-step recovery approach, no book that can help you move forward. But God—*God* will crown you with peace that surpasses all understanding as He carries you through such crippling storms.

The Lord is my shepherd; You are *covered* and *cared* for. I shall not want. *He's a provider.* He maketh me to lie down in green pastures: *He gives you rest.* He leadeth me beside the still waters. *He gives you peace.* He restoreth my soul: *He is a redeemer.* He leadeth me in the paths of righteousness for his name's sake. *You are His.* Yea, though I walk through the valley of the shadow of death, *Just trust Him.* I will fear no evil: *Just have faith.* For thou art with me; *He will never leave or forsake you.* Thy rod and thy staff they comfort me. *He loves you.* Thou preparest a table before me in the presence of mine enemies: *He will establish you.* Thou anointest my head with oil; *He will bless you.* My cup runneth over. *He will give you more than enough.* Surely goodness and mercy shall follow me. *That's favor.* All the days of my life: and I will dwell in the house of the Lord for ever—*That's eternal love*

CHAPTER 5

Twister

Many are the afflictions of the righteous, but God delivers us from them all. No matter what storm you face—a relationship, the home, a job or at church—know that God will not place more on you than you can bare. The pain is the evidence that you are growing. God is shaping and making you. We may not always understand God's reasoning for allowing certain things to take place in our lives, but His thinking is above and beyond our thinking. Just wait on the Lord—He is the boss. If you feel like you have been forgotten, hold on to the promise that says those who are last shall be first. *You are next in line for a miracle!*

In my life, I have gone through some trials in the workplace that caused me to second-guess myself. After all, we must always examine inwardly with a humble countenance. As my spiritual eyes grew attentive to the Holy Spirit, I began to witness the truth about spiritual wickedness in high places, where no one is exempt. Don't take these setbacks personally; just pray and God will make your enemy your footstool. The Twister…it was one *ugly* storm.

For several years in my life, I worked as a contract employee for various temporary agencies. Some of the assignments were short term, but most were long term. I figured I was making decent money and would always have work, right? Wrong! There came a dry spell—I was so discouraged while in the wilderness. My bills kept growing and I was sinking in them. I was beat up and my spirit beat down. I was afraid that I would be homeless, without my car, you name it.

To be honest, at the time I was questioning God. I wanted to know why He would dry up every avenue I pursued in a city as plentiful as Manhattan. All my friends were working, but I could not get work despite the fact that I had solid relationships with New York City head-hunters. I had the skills, the experience, the talent—even a collection of power suits! One time in particular stands out: I called for work and the company had nothing. Within moments, a friend of mine called the same company and got work instantly. When I called our recruiter, she said, "It was a fluke. Your friend called at the same time we were receiving an urgent request for a temp. Her timing was just lucky." At the time I was active in my church, singing in the choir, inviting folks to service, etc. The word "WHY" was in every sentence that came out of my mouth. At the end of the day after all is said and done, God knows best, and is never the less in control. He is our redeemer!

I guess God knew something that I didn't, so God pulled me out of Manhattan. A year, one month, and two days later, September

11th would shake the city and the world with a tragic event that could have changed my destiny. When things seem hard and the odds seem to be against you, cry to the hills for help-- divine help is on the way. Tough it out and know that God is God.

As a result of the closing doors in New York, I began to apply for permanent positions, which would afford job security. This would be easy enough, I assumed. The problem was, every time I interviewed, employers kept asking why I freelanced so long. Because temps appear flighty, they assumed I couldn't handle full-time work. No matter how hard I tried to convey that I was reliable and responsible, the end result was the same: no consideration available until I could gain more experience. This was so frustrating and unfair—I needed someone to give me a chance.

I started praying and praying and praying through this drought, asking the leaders in my church to pray for me. A friend of mine suggested that I apply to her company, which was based out of New Jersey, where I happened to be living at the time. I interviewed with this corporation, and although I was not hired for that particular job, I want you to see how God's hand helped move me on the correct path. During that interview, the Hiring Recruiter and I made a personal connection. It seemed as though there was a heavenly bridge that formed between us. Does not a bridge have a purpose? I learned later that a few weeks after our interview, the HR Manager was cleaning her office and decided to take boxes of files home to store them in her garage. She dropped one of the boxes and several papers fell out. As she began picking them up, her eyes rested on my resume. She began to read it, and was reminded of a position available under the Senior Vice President of Human Resources. So she took the resume into the office the next morning to invite me for an interview. Now it was all up to me to make the most of the opportunity God gave me.

During this new interview, it was as if God spoke for me. Though I was pretty well seasoned for the corporate arena and had acquired strong interviewing skills, I found myself speaking as though I were an interview strategist.

The Hiring Manager opened with the routine question, "Tell me why you have been temping for so long?"

I felt my eyes stretch but only slightly. Then suddenly calm came over me and I opened my mouth: "During my experiences as a consultant I was able to leverage a unique application of skills that one could only acquire through being on-board at multiple top companies with a track record of documented successes. I have been afforded the opportunity to step into some of the strongest and most powerful firms who were presented with immediate need for a project leader who could align initiatives with the organizations' overall mission. I've received nothing short of the best experience in hands on education, particularly thru the flexibility of contracting and consulting for such industry leaders. This is why I targeted long and short term projects in the capacity of a consultant or a temp if you will—because the transferable knowledge and experience gained, has proven invaluable and has contributed to my confidence in knowing that I can hit the platform running in any new and challenging scenario."

As I spoke, I could feel the spirit of God guiding my tongue. I saw that God will open doors for you and he will make provisions for you. He will cover you with favor and make you an irresistible radiant light. The only thing that stands between you and victory is the effects of fear at play. When God says yes, no man can say no. Walk with God and you will see that he is faithful and that he cares for you. We take far too much credit in general, for stuff that He works out on our behalf. It is a good thing when you are heavily connected, so that God has the opportunity to bless your through other people. Understand that though the very same people may desire to block you, but the more people you know, the more opportunity God has to turn hearts towards you. When you are HEAVENLY connected, it's a done deal. Be reminded that we are peculiar creatures and the light that shines forth in us is contagious and captivating. God loves you-- He is warring for you. Let Him fight the battle for you. Just show up in Faith and He will show out on your behalf. Be confident in knowing that your Daddy is in charge and He has a soft spot just for you. So guess what happened? My Daddy gave me that job.

> *But we have this treasure in earthen vessels that the excellence of the power may be of God and not of us. We are hard-pressed on every side, yet not crushed; we are perplexed, but not in despair; persecuted, but not forsaken; struck down, but not destroyed. Therefore we do not lose heart. Even though our outward man is perishing, yet the inward man is being renewed day by day. For our light affliction, which is but for a moment, is working for us a far more exceeding and eternal weight of glory, while we do not look at the things which are seen, but at the things which are not seen. For the things which are seen are temporary, but the things which are not seen are eternal.* [2 Corinthians 4:7-18]

Thinking back on the day of the interview, I can remember

getting dressed in one of those trusty power suits. I selected a grey tweed skirt suit. But as I went to try on the suit I discovered that it was a bit snug. I was determined to wear it because it was "that suit." I asked my husband how I looked and he said I was fine. Of the two positions available working under the Senior Vice President, one had been filled, and I was nervous and wanted to make a good impression. After interviewing me, the VP himself made a bait and switch. He gave me the higher position, the one that was filled, in spite of my long haul as a temp. I started the job and received favorable feedback from HR and various associates: they were very pleased with my performance and glad I had joined the company. This was nice to hear.

As the weeks advanced, I noticed my clothes were getting tighter and tighter. I thought about dieting and joining the gym; after all, the gym was on-site. One day after work a friend was moving and asked me and my husband to lend a hand. Later that night I started spotting—this went on for about nine days. My husband and I scheduled an appointment with my doctor. I figured my system was shifting as I got older. Not so.

"You're pregnant!" The doctor said.

"Huh?"

He repeated it. "You guys are pregnant."

"How!?" We were completely blindsided.

"You are pregnant, and at this point it is 50/50 whether or not you'll make it to full term."

I was so unprepared for this one. Here I was thirty-four years old and a new employee in a demanding job. I decided since the chance was 50/50, I would simply wait before I made any announcements. Four months went by before I knew it and I was beginning to show. I remembered the question during the interview, *"Soooo…Sonya, are you planning on having any more children?"* I had confidently answered, "No, we are all set, and it is not in our plans." How many times has God's plan been different from your plans? A billion times…that is why we must simply surrender to His perfect will and plan for our life.

Remembering my confident "No" I instantly felt guilty, afraid, and hypocritical. The enemy took over through fear and ran rampant in my thoughts each day. I was growing in my physical body with a wonderful gift, but shrinking in my spirit and confidence day by day. The law said I didn't have to say a word, but would that really be wise? I was about five months along when I entered my boss's office and broke the news. He smiled gallantly. "Mazal Tov!"

"Mazal Tov?" I asked

"Yes," he replied. "That means congrats."

I figured this was easy enough. I felt like I had put myself through unnecessary anxiety. The very next day he called me into his office and announced that things were not working out. When he said this, he had the very same smile fixed upon his face as the day before. I nearly choked; this was news opposite the rave reviews I'd been receiving prior to my announcement. He demoted me and placed me in an itsy bitsy cubicle in the hallway on another floor away from his organization. It was obvious that he wanted me to throw in the towel. As I became very pregnant, I could hardly turn my chair from left to right inside my cubicle. I had to roll out backwards to exit—no exaggeration. He gave me mindless assignments and hardly said hello to me when I would see him in passing. I saw him on the elevator and it was as if we never met. His behavior, coupled with the unexpected loss of my grandmother, put too much stress on my body, and I went into early labor before I reached my third trimester.

I remember after my grandmother's funeral, and afterwards how difficult returning to work was for me. I was very close to my grandmother—she was my buddy. I would call her for advice, recipes, you name it, and she would call every single day to check on me and tell me she loved me. There were times when I walked in from work and dinner was just about ready for the kids. The curtains were changed, the linen was fresh, and I may have even had a new piece of furniture. Grandma gave to everyone and had issues with accepting from others. She worked at a nursing home from 11PM to 7AM and she would somehow wind up at my house, trying to help me out with my chores, after a full night shift—can you imagine? Ethel Woods just kept going and going, it was all she knew.

Her husband—my grandfather—passed away in September of 1981. They had many years together and three children together: my Mom and two sons. My grandfather spoiled us rotten. It would take me forever to tell you all about my wonderful angels called Grandma and Grandpa, but I can tell you Grandpa was a contractor with his own business. One of the ventures they shared successfully was Wood's Christmas Trees. Every December they would sell Christmas trees in town, as well as deer and ponies for the children to feed and ride. They would auction off these animals at the end of Christmas season. My grandfather donated trees to many of the town schools, churches and beyond.

Grandpa was a loving and giving man and very handsome. He had a beautiful smile and loved to dress up—he was sharp, and had matching hats for most of his suits. He would pull his hat to the side and stand in the doorway rocking back and forth, with his arms out at his side. He would ask of us, "Is Granddaddy sharp?"

We would run up to him and say "Yes, you are!" and get hugs and kisses in return. He was a very proud man and greatly respected in his community. Then one day in 1980 he became sick with cancer; after he died, Grandma never dated anyone again, instead she just focused on work and family. It was what she loved to do, and it was a gift from God.

Grandma was also supportive of her family back in Pennsylvania; she often sent money to them, helping with many bills and burdens for them—especially her older sister Rose. My grandmother was beautiful, sophisticated and polished, and so long as you didn't upset her flow, she was an angel (though this particular angel could pack her wings quite well in an instant, should she need to.) I myself made it my business to stay on her good side, as Mrs. Woods was a force to be reckoned with. As a young girl, I was once guilty of, as she called it, "sassing her." One moment I was in front of grandma and the next I was in the arms of a bull with my feet dangling just above ground.

"As long as you live don't you ever sass me like that again." She said, holding me with one trembling arm. I thought to myself, *no win in this one for me,* so it was "yes ma'am" or "no ma'am" for the rest of my days. On another occasion of when my mother incurred my Grandma's wrath, Grandma smacked my forty-year-old mother with a newspaper for "talking back a little too much."

Grandma was something else, but her love ran deep and we knew she was absolutely in our corner. For years after Grandpa died, my grandmother and her kids maintained the Christmas tree business in his memory. He loved Christmas and the business meant so much to him. Year after year she would leave the nursing home at seven a.m., go home to shower and take a nap, before heading over to the Christmas tree lot to run her business with Uncle Ron. Sometimes my Mom and Uncle Jim pitched in. Grandma did this without flinching—she never missed a day at work or complained. But the Christmas of 1999 was different. Grandma began to move slower than usual and seemed to have no fight in her. She even called off work a night or two. I called her and told her I was coming to see her. She asked me to bring her some citrate magnesium, which I did, along with dinner. When I arrived she could not eat. She drank two bottles of the citrate, but nothing.

The morning after Christmas, Uncle Ronnie called us and said that Grandma had been admitted into the hospital, and they were running all kinds of test. My sister lived in Maryland, but she and her husband drove up straight away. She had never been sick before and if she was admitted, we figured there had to be a serious problem. We all rushed over to see about her. She was up laughing and talking and seemed just fine. Everyone was confident that she was fine. At some point my husband asked the family to pray while we were waiting for test results. We prayed together. We shared so many old stories together.

Eventually everyone left the room for various reasons, leaving Grandma, my husband Cecil, and me. She asked me about my baby and if I had picked out a name yet. I told her we were having a boy, and my husband said, "We plan to name him Silva Bernard Ward, as Bernard is my middle name."

"I wanted to name him Silva Storm," I said, "Because I met his dad on the day of a huge snow-storm."

Grandma straightened her shoulders and said, "Wait a minute. Wait, wait, wait—name him what his Dad wants. Bernard, after him." Grandma believed in passing the names around. So we decided to name our son Silva Bernard, just like Grandma said. She thanked my husband for being a wonderful person and putting up with her granddaughter as she chuckled.

Grandma asked Cecil to read the Bible to her as she, in a child-like manner followed along, piecing the stories together as if she was hearing them for the first time. Then she talked about what she called the "strangest dream" she had ever had. In the dream she saw her car breaking down at the bottom of a hill. In the dream she telephoned Uncle Ron to come get the car. She claimed Uncle Ron didn't want her to leave the car; he said "Ma, just wait until I get there." Grandma said then a well-dressed man showed up by the car; she was happy to see him, so she graciously walked with him to the top of the hill. Once she got to the top, she looked back at her broken car and just shrugged her shoulders, continuing on her way, leaving the car behind.

It made me feel uneasy as I recalled the gift that my grandmother had possessed, being the seventh child born with a veil over her eyes. She had prophetic visions, and this made my soul shake. I left the room because I did not want her to see me crying. When I came back in my husband was praying the confession prayer with her and I got even more upset.

"Why are you praying that prayer, what are you doing?" I demanded. I was frantic deep inside, but I choked back my tears for Grandma, who was peaceful and confident in whatever came to pass. Now, I can see that the car represented her body, and the hill represented her service. The shrugging shoulders, perhaps, would be her surrender and faith, and the man her savior. For Grandma, it was all well with her soul.

Soon everyone returned to the room and the doctor came with the test results. Grandma had an aneurism lodged between her lung and her heart that would require surgery immediately. The doctor said because of the operation's difficulty (due to the location of this aneurism), she would be transferred to a hospital better equipped to handle such a tedious procedure. They transferred Grandma, and everyone followed the ambulance; we did not want to leave her alone.

We figured that I should go home and rest while Mom and my sister would stay with Grandma at the hospital overnight. I remember leaving the hospital feeling like I was in a bubble. It seemed to me nobody was getting it—I knew that my grandmother's journey was commencing and they didn't seem to understand. My siblings stayed and I left. I cried most of the night, waking up and at seven-thirty-seven a.m.

I called my Dad. "My grandmother is dying," I told him.

"Why would you say that? Her surgery will go just fine." He tried to calm me. "Have faith, trust God and His will."

I got out of bed to go to the hospital and relieve the others. Then my phone rang, and my brother said, "We are all meeting at James' house."

"Why? I am going to sit with Grandma."

"No," he said. "Come here, and we will all go together." When I arrived, they told me she was gone. I didn't understand

"Where'd she go?"

"She died at 7:30 this morning. The hospital called Uncle Ronny to tell him. My siblings didn't want me to go there by myself to find out. The nurse said she sat up and said she was in pain in her chest and she just collapsed."

This was too much, way too much for me. I made it through the funeral, but within the next couple of days, I was in labor. It seemed once I went into labor, it never stopped, but kept happening over and over again. I would be given medicine to stop the labor, then a few days later, the pangs would start again. My husband and I became regulars it seemed at St. Barneys within that two-month window (five to seven months)—and the nursing staff knew us well. I remember a particular visit clearly because I was at work when I called my husband and told him he needed to take me to the hospital. When I arrived I was in labor again. They tried medications to stop the labor, but when my body didn't respond, the nurse prepped me for delivery as a precaution. At that time I was in the six-month window, which was still risky for the baby. They felt that he needed to gain more weight and his lungs particularly needed to develop, so they started steroidal treatment. I was so scared and in so much pain it was like a nightmare.

The nurse came into the room with a cordless phone and handed it to me, saying "You have an important phone call." *This is odd,* I thought to myself as I took the phone. It was my boss asking how I was.

"I'm in labor," I panted.

Without missing a beat, he said, "Do you think you will be in tomorrow to address some open projects, or is it real?"

I looked at the phone in shock, not knowing if he was clueless or simply ruthless. At that point my husband took the phone and ended the call. The labor stopped and I was released the next day to strict bed rest. I was fearful of losing my job, the salary and the benefits— we could not make it on my husband's salary alone. Rather than honing in on my present situation, I fast-forwarded to the future, allowing my own thoughts to cloud my judgment. I allowed the possibilities of losing my job to dictate what was actually going on and what mattered most, our baby. As a result I later wound up spending a week in cardiology as well.

No matter what happened, I was in God's hands and we would have been just fine with or without that job. No man can shut the door God opens. When we stop making a mess for ourselves, He gets us back on track and things work out for the good. At that time I was foolish and I was not grounded. I had a stressful job, a sadistic boss, and I was an emotional wreck. So when my husband left for work, after kissing me and telling me to stay off my feet, I got dressed and went to work. Fear was my boss.

Our son Silva Bernard was born in my seventh month of pregnancy, healthy thank God, and weighing five pounds three ounces. He was a beautiful little fellow. When I returned to work from Maternity Leave, I had no work-space, no assignment, no boss allegedly. I stood around for the entire day just kind of drifting. The next day my former boss and I had an annual review. Needless to say, the games began. His mouth was the deadly weapon and I was the target. I remember feeling a major wave of heat across my face as I sat there and struggled for air. I felt as if the room was closing in on me and spinning all at once. I literally could not breathe normally. The heat that flushed under my skin was nothing I'd ever felt before. I could literally hear my heart beating in my ears and head at the same time. I remember fighting back tears from major shock at the things he documented against me. I glanced at him as I read the words, only to discover his glee as he watched me read his overview of my performance. But as I mentioned earlier, no one is exempt and this is a snapshot of what the enemy will do. He will pervert your canvas and falsely accuse you. Satan is an accuser, an accuser of the gospel of Jesus Christ and those who follow Him.

I looked up at my boss and noted that he was leaning back in the chair of this conference room, chewing gum like a happy-go-lucky lark, the same plastic smile stretched across his face. He had his feet up on the table in this conference room with no shoes on—he was famous for that. He had his arms folded above his head as he watched my every expression. What did I do to deserve this? Was I guilty of any of this? No, no way, this was fabricated. I was guilty of one thing, guilty of being pregnant. God knows I honestly did not know or anticipate this miracle pregnancy. So technically I was innocent. For you as you read this book, think about this: how many times have you been under attack and wrongly accused? An attack against your character, your persona, your spirit, your joy, your love, your livelihood, your mission!? The enemy will come from all angles to tear you up and tear you down...but the Holy Spirit will guide you, direct you, protect you, deliver you, lift you up, make your enemies your footstool, set you on high and fight for you! I said fight **For** you; in other words, fight on **Your** behalf. We must learn our roles in every event and know how to pick and choose. *This is not your fight, and it was not mine, this is something for Jesus to handle!*

HE WILL TEACH YOUR HANDS TO WAR.

My boss had gotten others to back up his story. Corporate Resolutions and many of the associates joined him to witness against me. They collaborated in orchestrating the demise of my professional character within that organization. Now, I could have easily dusted off my coat and moved on, for my God can plant me and have me to prosper anywhere He predestines. The enemy worked to make me look bad, but God in His infinite wisdom showed me every scheme that was being plotted against me. I was always a step ahead in the scheme of things, so when all was said and done, I was vindicated in Jesus. Here's what God says concerning the arrows that fly by noonday:

> *You give your mouth to evil, and your tongue frames deceit. You sit and speak against your brother; you slander your own mother's son. These things you have done and I kept silent; you thought that I was altogether like you; but I will rebuke you, and set them in order before your eyes" "Now consider this, you who forget God, lest I tear you in pieces, and there be none*

to deliver: Whoever offers praise glorifies Me; and to him
who orders his conduct aright I will show the salvation
of God. [Psalm 50:19-23]

Friend of mine, this was one year into my tenure with this company, and I stayed there for all of seven years before it was said and done. I was there because God planted me there with His favor. I stayed because God covered me and protected me from dangers seen and unseen. When I left it was because God had something greater for me. Never question when God is shutting a door, in doing so he may be ushering change that will bless you. We don't always feel the quiet nudge along the way so we stay a little longer than advised. Then too, in the eye of the beholder, is our view on the overall picture. In the seventh year, the door was gently closed and I heard the quiet nudge. In trust, I marched on and in faith, I stood in anticipation and at birth, I received new blessings. You see, we are not called to be stagnant people. We are called to be like Christ and He is not in a box. He has not fashioned us to fear that in a person place or thing is the end all be all. He is the all and all. He is everywhere, making things happen.

Yes, you may find yourself in the dark entrapment of the jaws of the whale, Jonah, but had you heeded the nudge, you would not be there. He has a plan! Listen! Listen for the voice of your Father. Get to know Him and His voice, so when He moves, you are in position. In a dance one leads the other follows, less you stumble at your feet. Dance in sync and sing harmonically, it's so much better. Although this is not always the case, in the outcome, I was able to see the results of the attack concerning the corporate posse. I witnessed first hand how my Redeemer vindicated me. When folks plot to destroy in haste they make multiple mistakes, which expose them in their messy attempts to hurt you. Such divisors. They forgot about the truth, omitting my true profile mischaracterizing me. My Daddy did not like that at all. He is not going to let anyone harm you. He gave all free will, so they can act up and mess up their own blessings because it is their personal will, to do so. But God! God comes to rescue those who speak praises and truth over his servants. But when you lie on a saint, you have lied before God. The reward for evil works? The terror of the night and the arrow that flies at noon-day. Such spiritual criminals will not be spared from the fowler's snare. In the word of God we are reminded that He will rebuke and tear to pieces those who slander or speak evil of their brother. Remember there is a rod and a staff. Surely! Surely! Surely goodness AND mercy shall follow you all the days of your life! SURELY God will turn things around. He will give back what the locust stole and what the enemy meant for bad God will turn around for good. Don't allow the cloud of distraction to blind you beyond your faith. Know that no matter how high the storm rages God is still in control.

But let patience have her perfect work, endure until the end that you may be perfect and entire, wanting nothing. God's promises are inherited through faith and patience [Hebrews 6:12] it's going to work in your favor! God is just! He will make the crooked places straight and you will bare witness to this, eventually. Not in your time but in His time. He has been with me through it all. You will notice this as you look back over your life, you never really go it alone. He will deliver us from the afflictions that are fashioned to destroy our destiny. His grace has proven to be sufficient time and time again! He never fails! Sing with me...

When you walk through a storm, hold your head up high and don't be afraid of the dark. At the end of the storm is a golden sky and a sweet silver song of a lark. Walk on thru the wind walk on thru the rain, though your dreams may be tossed and blown. Walk on walk on with hope in your heart and you'll NEVER walk alone, you will NEVER walk alone.

— Rogers and Hammerstein

Now understand something, this is the organized spiritual wickedness in high places that you have been hearing and reading about. By now, you've probably witnessed some of it. This war was not about flesh and blood, rather an outward violent attack against ones spirit. It was an attack against the spirit that dwells inwardly. God planted seeds in every one of us. The enemy is angry about this and he doesn't want you to discover the truth about who you are in Jesus. God has planted greatness in you and fashioned you in His likeness, with **wonder working** power. That you may bare witness, being an epistle seen and read of all men, that is able to do exceeding and abundant great things. The enemy never wants you to water these seeds. He wants them to dry up on spoiled ground. But when you start tapping the power within, you activate the Christ in you. In doing so, you water those seeds by God's spirit and by your Faith. You release your purpose into the hands of your destiny and begin to soar in triumph. You do all this by reading, meditating and living by God's Word. He has given the gift of His Holy Spirit, and the truth is that this particular gift is a problem for the enemy of your soul.

> The Lord had said to Abram, *"Leave your country, your people and your father's household and go to the land I will show you. I will make you into a great nation and I will bless you; I will make your name great, and you will be a blessing. I will bless those who bless you, and*

79

*whoever curses you I will curse; and all peoples on earth
will be blessed through you."* [Genesis 12: 1-3]

God wants to know that you continue to trust Him in the midst
of your trial. The question is, *can you lift up holy hands, when the
tides are high?* There is power in your praise and wonder in your
worship! Just like the footprints in the sand, you will find that in
your most difficult times, *"it was then that He carried you."* Don't
allow the enemy to tell you that-- those are just phrases, mere words.
Meditate on that which is good and pure. Keep your mind stayed
on Thee and, a wonderful change will come over you. **God is true
and marvelous!** The enemy hates when you are lining up with Gods
will and your purpose. He will fight you and send distractions to
drain you so that you can't go forward. He wants to shut up your
praise and interrupt your hour of worship. So long as you are living
your will, you are not a threat to him. But when you straighten up
and begin to fly right, he comes, like a thief in the night, plotting to
steal, kill and destroy. HIS Will is your WAY out of no way, it is your
ticket to eternal life and endless joy! It's your road to resolution. It
is your transfer from victim to victor! It is your bridge over trouble-
some waters. God's will is how you triumph over every trial! It is
always the solution and never the problem. The Word of God says
resist the evil one and he/she will flee. Know that his arms are too
short to box with God. In your life God will require that you stand
or about face from a particular situation. This is why it is of utmost
importance that you become sensitive in the spirit: so that you gain
enough spiritual sense, to enable clarity in the supernatural realm.
You need to be able to hear God and receive His guidance.

*Who is like the wise man? Who knows the explanation
of things? Wisdom brightens a man's face and changes*

its hard appearance. Obey the king's command, I say, because you took an oath before God. Do not be in a hurry to leave the king's presence. Do not stand up for a bad cause, for he will do whatever he pleases. Since a king's word is supreme, who can say to him, "What are you doing?" Whoever obeys his command will come to no harm, and the wise heart will know the proper time and procedure. For there is a proper time and procedure for every matter, though a man's misery weighs heavily upon him. Since no man knows the future, who can tell him what is to come? No man has power over the wind to contain it; so no one has power over the day of his death. As no one is discharged in time of war, so wickedness will not release those who practice it. [Ecclesiastes 8:1-8]

If you fear God, you will not have to live in fear. When you know Him and honor him, you know who you are and what is wise versus what is plain foolishness. Get your house right. In doing so you live in the peace and confidence in knowing that you are covered, cared for and chosen.

When people hurt you, you are required to do one thing and that is to love them, praise God and keep on keeping on. Get still and anchor yourself in the Word and in God's unfailing love. I guarantee you that

You will not bare guilt as a result of self vindication.

You will not lose sleep as a result of making a god out of your pressing situation.

You will be better than blessed for taking the high road through worship rather than the alley ways through curse-ship.

Most often you are being strengthened through circumstance and failing only means you must repeat this test yet again. He knows your heart and He can see every move you make: good, bad, and indifferent. God says that wisdom brightens a man's face and changes its hard appearance. A wise man is not easily provoked. If you are easily provoked you might want to pray for God to grant you in increase in the area of wisdom. Surrender here and now, so that the God of Abraham, Isaac, and Jacob can do what He does best. "Fear Not" in your trial, because God is in there with you through it all. He will take care of you. He will set you where you ought to be. Fear not! Only trust Him!

CHAPTER 6

Whirlwind

O f all storms I have endured, the most complex for me would be spiritual brokenness. Often with troubles, we go to God indirectly through elders and ministers, seeking direction or help. But where do you go when it is the people of God, or the so-called people of God who have spun the web that has broken your wings? While there is value in every valley, there too, is value in every storm. It's just hard to see it that way. A spiritual storm has several entrances but only one exit. The only way out is through God. Such a storm will force you to your own knees praying yourself through, going directly to the true source. I call this "the whirlwind" because it forced me to travel the road that led to the development of a true relationship with God, though I was surrounded by chaos and confusion. In life, as you begin to go forward—journeying towards your purpose, you will need the power to march on.

What you have to do is remember that man is man and God is

God. Keep your eyes on God and allow his guiding spirit to be the compass by which you go forth. It is less disappointing and holds great promise. I pray that you understand that your test is your storm. Remember the sparrow—Go in faith!

First get this in your *ready spirit;* its quite relevant:

> *For though we walk in the flesh, we do not war according to the flesh. for the weapons of our warfare are not carnal* **but mighty through God** *for pulling down of strongholds, casting down arguments and every high thing that exalts itself against the knowledge of God, bringing every thought into captivity to the* **obedience of Christ.**
> [Ephesians 6:12]

I remember being young, very young, perhaps seven years old. We lived on High Street, the park where we played was on High Street, the school we attended was on High Street, the Church where we worshiped was on High Street—even the candy store was on High Street. It was a nice neighborhood: safe, comfortable, everything quite convenient. So it was not uncommon for me to go to the corner store alone, or walk to school by myself.

Trinity Presbyterian Church is positioned on the corner of High Street and Orange Road. The presiding Pastor was the late Reverend Reginald McGhee. This was our family church and, in fact, it is where many of our family members attend today. In this building my relatives have been married, my nieces and nephews baptized, my grandparents and mother laid to rest. As a child I was always curious about church—the Word of God and the music ministry. I was drawn there, independent of invitation. I would get up on Sunday morning and dress myself, then walk myself to the church. It seems dangerous now, but at the time it was safe: the church was close by and I knew everyone. I would meet up with my cousin Marva-Jean (she later changed her name to Tauheedah). In my mind, the service was not colorful at all; I kept getting pinched by various church mothers for falling asleep. I was unsure as to what kept drawing me to church. As my grandmother used to say, "every shuteye ain't sleep," and she was right: though I fell asleep, I still somehow got fed through the Word.

As I got older, I discovered St. Paul's Baptist Church, just two blocks away on Elm Street. I had a friend named Marcel Noel that invited me there. Her father was a deacon, so I joined them on Sunday's for service. Gail Freeman directed the choir. She was amazing to me. Gail used to sing "He is that Kind of Friend," and I would cry every time she wailed about her friend Jesus, a friend closer than any brother or sister. *"If you ever need a friend that will stick closer than any brother, any brother, I recommend Jesus, Jesus, because He is that kind of friend. He walks right in front of you, He will always protect you, so the devil can do you no harm. If within your heart you take Him in, a new life will begin, because He is that kind of friend!"* I heard every word in that song. It ministered to my young mind and made me want to help others as well. I auditioned for the choir as soon as I could. I was so excited to be a part of this praise ministry. I attended this church for a couple of months and found the services to be powerful and the members loving. At twelve I was baptized there. However, I was unable to continue membership at St. Paul's; just a few weeks later, we moved to another city when my parents separated.

Mommy wanted to do something new, so we moved to East

Orange, into what Mommy called a "Luxury high-rise apartment building." She was so excited about this place. There were kids of all ages and varying backgrounds throughout this building. I met Judea Yvette Freeman, whose mother and aunties were evangelist, prayer warriors, and prophets. This was all new to me, especially the idea of the prophetic ministers. The closest I'd come to this intensity in worship was when I'd visit my Nana's church during summer visits to Greensboro. Another apartment neighbor was Rhoda Phillips Daniels, whose father was a pastor. Between these two households, I saw things I'd never heard of or witnessed before.

I attended church with Rhoda and experienced worship service in such a powerful way, words can't explain. This was a store-front church, long and narrow. There you would find tambourines for instruments and stomping feet and clapping in sync for rhythm. The enthusiasm for God in that house was incredible. If you are talking about "Down Home Worship," they had it. This congregation was on fire for Jesus. For me this was so different from Trinity and St. Paul's, so much stronger in terms of personal experience with God. My first visit, I was not really sure why I was praising God, but I knew it felt like a very secure place and so I chimed in. I felt a sense of freedom and joy unexplainable. I knew I wanted a relationship with my Father, a true relationship.

I began to play with Judea, and we used to attend church with her Mom. The experience was very different than my experience with Rhoda's family. I can recall seeing them call out an unclean spirit. I was very uncomfortable, even confused—I couldn't remember how I had arrived there, but I wanted to leave. It was scary, I somehow felt safe after all, Judea's Mom, Ms. Jerry was brave and filled with the Spirit—if ever you needed some sure, powerful prayer, she was the one to help you. Yet all the same, I backed off somewhat spooked.

For a girl of twelve, this was a lot to take in, and I just was not prepared for all of this. Although my Nana taught me many hymns and prayers during our summers in Greensboro, the foundation was not consistent enough for me to erect a strong faith. I was quickly moved from a quietly polite church to a Baptist church to a Holiness church to a blazing-with-power experience in a little over a year. My mind was spinning with all I had seen and learned.

A couple years went by, and eventually our family moved back to Montclair. At the time I was almost 15, not really going to church, but I agreed to accompany a few of my friends to a new church they had discovered. In this I can offer that no matter where you are, if you are chosen by God, you will wind up where He wants you to be. We entered the edifice, and within ten minutes all the doors were shut. We were instructed to circle around the walls of the church and join hands. Just as with Judea's church, there was an unclean spirit in the building, and just like before, I wanted to leave. We were instructed to pray, to plead the blood of Jesus. We were informed that there was no time to be weak because the evil spirit could jump on the weakest one. I panicked, thinking, *How do I know that's not me?!* I was terrified, but all the same, I began to pray and call out, "The blood, the blood of Jesus is against you!" I remembered how Ms. Jerry prayed at the church in East Orange, so I drew from that experience. I had learned how to plead the blood of Jesus! Can I tell you that Experience is a great teacher? Later when I went home, I opened my bible, recalling how powerless I had felt because of the fear that had risen up in me. I wanted the Lord to show me how I could become better equipped on my own to handle fear.

This was a turning point in my life—my priorities began to shift towards school, away from church. I got involved in school activities, talent shows and pageants. These character-building opportunities took a great deal of time and so, somewhere along the line I put my bible on the shelf. A part of me felt like religion was so frightening, that I just would rather not "for now." Having always loved people and showmanship, I became a cheerleader. I won a couple of competitions, not realizing that the special spark I seemed to have was not coming from my garment, hair style, voice, or c-jump, but rather from my Father. It is always God giving us that extra push and that extra lift, that special something. This is why it is so important to lay a foundation and teach your children so they have that Rock to stand on and that salvation to live by.

I came from a musical family that loved to perform. Everyone either played or sang or did something entertaining. My instrument is my voice. In high school, since I was not in a church choir, I sang in groups. When I went to college, my roommates were students from local Arts Magnets. Together we'd sing wherever we could to pass time—in the dorm room, hallways, student halls, cafeteria, you name it. Then I met the amazing Kevin Horton, who spent a great deal of time in the student center playing that grand piano. Kevin was like Rhoda—he looked and behaved differently, he spoke differently. Kevin prayed openly and He talked about God all the time. You could usually find him reading his bible. He taught me gospel songs, and I found myself in the zone of unspeakable joy.

Susan Lancaster was an upper classman with a strong alto voice and an old soul. A genuine and pure-hearted young lady, Susan was always offering scriptures to support what she advised. I'd like to think of her as That Ram, since God always has a Ram in the bush for His children. I wish I could have spent more time with them in college. But over the summer, during the cyclone in which I lost my dear friend Terri, school seemed impossible. I just couldn't focus. Luckily, my college friends and I still have lasting friendships.

I pursued a music career, got a full time job, and moved onward. I was quite busy living and not giving. I was not giving God my heart, my time or my attention. Now and then I would pray and read scriptures, but the true relationship was not being nurtured. At the time I was still seeing my college boyfriend. We courted for two years. I spent a great deal of time with him and his family—I loved his mother deeply. She taught me many things, including cooking and sewing, and was there for me on many levels. I was even close with his cousins; one chatterbox named Wanda—who the family endearingly refers to as "Mickey"—invited me to a church service at Christian Bible Center, under the very loving and anointed Dr. Donald Womack. Never one to turn down an invitation to church, I agreed.

It was amazing. During this service I remember praying and crying and thanking God for allowing me to be there and to praise Him. I felt Him covering me and protecting me. I also felt a rush in my stomach like a mild tornado spinning and circling around my waist. I had no idea that I was carrying my first child, my daughter Sonyae Elise. I was not married, a major blow, and I was living with two girlfriends—a breeding ground for error at such a tender age. During this service God, the one who has ways above and beyond our ways, knew what I didn't know. He knew that I was with child and I was lost. He knew when I didn't know, that my roommates would later try to convince me to abort due to my circumstances. He knew they would somehow convince me to go, that they would drive me there. And when I would see that eight-car accident, He would know that I saw his divine hand averting disaster. I share this to say He caught me when I was falling.

Later I joined that ministry and was with them for years to come. I was there up until the passing of Dr. Womack. I joined the praise team and I realized the importance of a heavenly relationship, so I became a student of the word. There I heard the gospel, I was taught, I witnessed and I was fed. I learned that through brokenness you could be made whole, and what comfort in knowing! I was just now getting the foundation to put the pieces together. For the first time, it all began to make sense to me.

Dr. Womack really was an angel in my life. Mightily gifted and specially anointed in the gifting of love, you could see love and joy pouring out of this man in such a peculiar and fascinating way. I thank God for him and the legacy he left in the hands of his family. Dr. Womack passed away during a conference in Pennsylvania, I believe. In the middle of a service, they say he was praying for folks and suddenly he lifted his hand high, looked up and smiled. Then he fell to the ground with an expression of peace and bliss. The joy on that man's face could only be rendered of God. I tell you God on the inside is miraculous overall.

After Dr. Womack passed, I stopped going to church for some years. I shacked with my boyfriend, the producer and, I should mention, a married man. He claimed he was going to get divorced, but after years together, he left me for the next young lady, also not his wife. He produced a couple of my (secular) songs that became records, and fathered our daughter, but other than that, he didn't leave me with much. He was kind enough to tell me however, that I had let myself go and that she—his new lover--was everything I once was, when he first met me. I began to think of the pain I must have caused his wife; the Lord allowed me to see myself, the undone filthy wretch I'd become. I knew better. What was I thinking, where was my sensitivity, where was my obedience? I didn't know what to do— he was my financial source, he was the man I loved.

Then there was Stella, my starlight! I met Stella during high school—she was popular, very pretty, a leader with a comedic edge about her. She was real, she shot from the hip but she was genuinely concerned about my soul. While I was going through this horrible break up, Stella happened to call me on a Sunday morning in December. I had been avoiding family and friends, in fact, when Stella called I was not answering my phone at all. I had picked up the receiver to call out, and there she was: "Hello." Usually I could conceal my emotions over the phone, but Stella could hear the desperation in my voice. She burst into a cry that shocked me—I never knew she loved me that much. Her purpose in calling had been to invite me to Faith Temple New Hope, her home church. I could not muster up an excuse, and before I knew it she had me in the car and on the way.

This was the first step towards reclaiming my life. The next thing I knew, I was back in the studio recording "You Took The Best Years." My anxiety had caused rapid weight loss—a little over fifty pounds—but my family rallied together to help me. My sister Charlotte would come over to make sure I was eating, and "Fearless James" would remind me, "Every flower that ever bloomed, had to go through a little dirt to get there!" I got a call for an audition for a girl group trio. The deal was already established—they just needed the girls—so I figured, "what's the harm?" After all, I could use the money, and the distraction. Stella kept saying that I needed to sing for God, but part of me felt like I had to prove I could record without my ex. I wanted to know for myself that I could do this.

Do you recall that wild snow storm from 1996? I will never forget that blizzard—a monster of a storm, yet very beautiful. I was supposed to meet up with my friend Dujour at DML Studios in East Orange, New Jersey. Joining us was Debbie, a singer from Jersey City, the producer Malik Pendleton, and Q, who at the time was an Epic recording artist. I was almost four hours late because of the condition of the roads, but luckily I arrived just in time. It was so cold outdoors we all bundled up inside over a pot of tea. Something about the savage beauty outside and the warmth inside caused me to open up to Q. Had the weather been finer, perhaps Q and I might never have had the chance to connect as we did. Q asked me if I was seeing anyone, and I told him the episode with my ex. "Don't worry," he said. "God counts and stores every tear." He told me that he was brought up Baptist, and that his father was once a Pastor. We began to hang out and write music, recording songs. Soon we were dating. Eventually our daughters met and became like sisters, the three of them. I could not help but notice that he was an amazing father.

I continued to visit Faith Temple New Hope. I invited Q and he came frequently. I joined the ministry, was once again baptized and eventually joined the choir. However, my past mistakes were a source of guilt which made me secretly feel undeserving of goodness. I purposed to stay connected and I found comfort in my ability to go to the elders for direction and prayer. On May 8, 1999 Q and I were married at Faith Temple New Hope. In March of 2000 our son Silva was born prematurely. As I mentioned before Silva, reminds me of the beautiful Silver Storm where Q and I met, while his name reminds my husband of being tried in the fire, yet coming out as pure gold. When I think of all, I agree with my husband. In life you experience fire and pain but it's all in the making, God is way ahead of us. He knows what we can't know.

I loved my church and I loved what God was doing in my life. I began to minister in praise and worship with other fellow saints. The testimonies were from one extreme to the next. They certainly spoke to my heart, helping me to see that I can escape my past by not living in it. This was indeed a process; it did not happen over night. I recall being at work, noticing that disgruntled employees began to approach me for counsel. Many issues were job related, but often they were not. Co-workers—often broken, hurt, or in tears—would come to me for prayer, and we'd pray together. I knew that God was getting me fit for something; I just didn't know what it was.

A minister from Faith Temple New Hope announced that God was calling him to build a ministry; my husband and I felt led to join him. I will advise that you pray before making these type decisions, because you don't want to move ahead of God. Sometimes He wants you to be still for a reason then release you in your season.

Everything seemed to line up with this decision: we found a home literally around the block from where service was being held, my commute was good, my husband found a job less than a mile away, and the kids adjusted to the school just fine.

The only problem was my health. Suddenly, I had joint pain everywhere, I ached severely—it was almost crippling. I was not ready for the approaching attack on my life, after already coming through so many other problems. I remember trying to reason with myself. I began to wonder if past sins were catching up with me; after all I had been selfish, and made some horrible decisions in my past. So I wavered between guilt and repentance, not sure which would overrule. Although I would repent, fear was lurking and that still small voice would play over in my mind guilty. Nonetheless I had the foundation, I had the word, I had a prayer life, I had elders, I had a praying husband--but I was not sure I had the intimacy with my Father that was independent of man.

I later learned that Anointing is something that comes from being broken virtually in every aspect and then made whole. Anointing is what takes your prayer life to new levels and breaks the yoke on the song you sing, it is what authorizes the direct connection; it is where access is granted and where you learn to walk by faith. Once you enter into these courtyards, you learn that the battle really is not yours but it is the Lord's. And so you begin to bind and release and you begin to recognize the birthing pains and you learn to push until purpose makes itself manifest. By now I had dropped another thirty-three pounds and experiencing night sweats so severe I had to change pajamas two to three times a night. I started using a cane to walk, suffering from blurred vision, joint pain, lethargy, and a persistent cough.

I tried to continue in my spiritual work. When I learned that my brother in-law had been diagnosed with sarcoidosis (something I'd never heard of) I began to research the illness to know how I should direct my prayers. As I studied this disorder, I began to realize that while he had three of the twelve symptoms, I actually had twelve of the twelve. I called my doctor, who scheduled me to be X-rayed. My lungs showed scarring, so my doctor immediately sent me to pulmonary specialist Dr. Jack Dadaian. Dr. Dadaian was a rare find: bright, quick, precautious, and willing to entertain holistic options in conjunction with modern medicine. He did a lung biopsy and sure enough, it was sarcoidosis, a "rare" debilitating disease. Within weeks, I discovered that a former Faith Temple minister, Pastor Paul, co-foundeder of Visions of God in partnership with his wife also battled sarcoidosis. I also discovered others who were suffering: my brother in-law, my sister in-law, my cousin Kim, her brother, cousin Joel, my friend Ty's ex, the nurse, a co-worker's brother, even the father of my hair stylist. So much for this being a rare disease!

As if this were not enough, my new boss did not respond to this very well. I went on disability and was admitted at The Wildwood Lifestyle Center (WWLSC) in Chattanooga, Tennessee, a Christian Alternative Healing Facility. There, the physicians pray for you concerning your health and your faith. When I arrived, I was using a cane and could barely walk. I remember how my husband would have to carry me to the bathroom because I could not get out of the bed. The WWLSC put me on a vegetarian diet, enforced daily exercise in spite of the pain, and provided various treatments such as contra, steam, and fever treatments. I had to have a fever treatment daily, the most difficult treatment to endure. Patients were submerged in a one-hundred-and-twenty degree whirlpool for forty-five minutes to induce a fever-like flush, promoting cell reparation. I was so sick from these induced fevers that I would vomit. I felt like I was slipping into an incoherent state during these treatments. This is why I love the promise of God that says "My strength is made perfect in your weakness:" although I was physically weak, I was spiritually strong. God ministered to me and kept me indeed. The only thing that got me through these aggressive treatments was God Himself. I would communicate with God in a heavenly tongue and then pass out. The staff did not believe in the utterance of tongues, as they were mostly Seventh Day Adventist. My nurse Olivia would sing to me, and found herself believing in this gift. Glory! I was there for seventeen days, I left there renewed holistically or I should say *holystically.*

I returned home on a Saturday in May of 2002. I was so happy to see my children, my Mom, and my husband. It seemed that I was away for six months; during the last days in treatment, I cried because I wanted to return to my family. My son was just two years old at the time, so you can imagine how difficult this was on everyone. I had barely put my bags in my room when my husband told me he wanted to talk about something. He explained that he had been moved in the spirit to do a new thing, and that he left our ministry a week prior to my return. I was devastated. I went for a walk in the park and consulted with my Father. He ministered to me, and it was sweet. He can make things just that way when you consult Him with your concerns.

Before I go further I want you to know that when life sends a storm that you can't see your way through pray the serenity prayer. Ask Him to give you the courage to change the things that you can. If you are going to be anything like, Christ, you have to become strong enough to war in the spiritual realm, you can't be afraid of every wind that blows your way. If you can peaceably resolve an issue, make Him proud and you will grow stronger with every success in this area of your life. Ask God to give you the wisdom to know the difference.

Sunday morning came and Cecil was getting ready for church. Though torn, I got dressed and joined him. This church was in its humble beginnings, so the service was held in the living room of the

Pastor's home. She was a married woman, but her husband never attended, choosing instead to stay in the bedroom. She had several cats and my daughter, who is highly allergic to cats, struggled through the service. The Pastor spoke briefly, then opened the door for souls to join the church. There were few members, perhaps six at best, all of which were women. This unfortunately is not uncommon, and I am praying for balance in this area. My husband's hands went up in the air and he cried out and joined. I froze in shock. I felt horrible that we had not discussed this in advance, but I was always one to reason with "the move in the spirit." The Pastor then asked will there be anyone else. This was meant for me, because all others were already members, besides me, my husband, and my young daughter. I didn't budge. This Pastor tilted her head down while looking up, shifting her hands from left to right.

"Now, now, now, now," she spoke at last. "We can't be unequally yoked! God would not have us to be divided, that is the spirit of rebellion and witchcraft. We can't be divided-- a house divided against it-self will surely fall." She went on with this for what seemed like hours but it was more like fifteen minutes. I never budged and never said a word. As I recall the sermon I don't really recall anything beyond her talking about the prophetic gift on her house, and her jumping up and down while screaming "Hey!", "Oh!", or "My God!" over and over. She closed the service by asking once again if anyone wanted to join her ministry. I was immobilized and was not released in my spirit, even a little bit, to join this ministry, so I was obedient and I thank God for that.

I did continue to visit with my husband with hopes that he would realize that he had jumped too soon, or that I would feel a release in my spirit, but Sunday after Sunday birthed no change. Each time I would visit, she would do the same thing at the end of the service, and she began to take personal offense regarding my indecision to join her ministry. I told her that it was not personal, and that I did not dislike her, but that I had to be guided by the Lord concerning such commitments. I promised her that I was praying about it, introspecting and so on.

Then came this day this one Sunday, when she prophetically lied, saying that God was going to bless me with permanent disability and that I would not work another day. I begin to war in my spirit and she began to jump and scream and shout about her supposed epiphany concerning my life. I worked full-time and enjoyed working, for the most part. Well the devil is a liar and the truth ain't in him, nor was it in her. This is why you have to pray and have a relationship with God, a true personal and intimate relationship. Be careful who you sit under, who speaks to your spirit man, who prays for you and lays hands on you and your marriage and your children and your destiny, because they will sift you as wheat if you're open. And they will do it all and seal it "in Jesus name." This is what the word means when it says do not use Jesus name in vain. Do not use it for your own will and tools to manipulate and twist the mind of others.

I think about two Sundays went by when my husband was honored for being the Head Prophet of this house. In the Pentecostal faith, offices can be ordained and appointed by the leader, and by the fourth Sunday the Pastor announced that my husband was now the Assistant Pastor. My husband was so pleased with what "God was doing" in his life. While I know that my husband is mightily gifted, a true prophet, heavily anointed and appointed to do a great work, this was happening all so fast. In support of my husband's zeal for God I suggested that he couple his call with seminary enrollment. In response to my advice, the Pastor suggested that I was jealous of my husband's gifts, his call, and his elevation—that I wanted to discredit him by sending him to a school that was no higher than God himself. I was furious.

On the Sunday when my husband was called as Assistant Pastor, he was schedule to speak in the second service. Upon completion of the first service, he went into the rest room to change his damp shirt. I was holding my toddler, waiting for my husband to come out, when the Pastor touched my shoulder and gestured me to the front door. She said, "Why don't you just go home and be a Mother to your children? Go take care of your babies." Then she shut the door.

I waited for a while and finally my husband came out. He asked what was wrong, and I shared the event.

"I absolutely cannot believe it," he said. "It is dangerous to lie about an apostle of God. You should be careful." He warned me that God would lay me flat on my back if I didn't stop. I got into the car and drove home, too angry to cry.

The phone rang within the hour. My husband called, saying the spirit of the Lord would not allow him to participate in the service, for the Lord showed him that his wife was telling the truth and he needed to repent.

"May I have your forgiveness?" He asked. I accepted.

On Monday the Pastor called me at work to apologize for her behavior, asking if we could start over. I agreed, but in the next breath she said, "Allow me to wash your clothes and cook for you, I desire to help. You are not well—let me help."

Instantly I could smell the rat. I knew that God had blessed me with assured gifts early on, but I just didn't understand how important they were. Every gift has been ordained to complete work that will take root in those who are in need, *even unto the gifted one.* I thank God for my gifts. Thank Him for your gifts. He has given me a discerning spirit. I thank God for the Holy Ghost. It will guide you and tug you and protect you.

I told her that this is an unnecessary gesture, and I appreciate her apology, but I needed to get back to work. I told my husband and he saw this as good, but not me....I knew the rat was playing dead. It was playing dead to her mission to destroy our union.

Over the past four weeks my husband had been constantly on the phone in prayer with one of the women (a prophetess) and the Pastor: in the morning, during dinner, while I lay beside him in bed. It was disturbing to my spirit and I felt deliberately disrespected. We began to argue, and our marriage began to suffer many blows. This Pastor as much as advised that my husband should not work, he should be in full-time ministry. That is of course (as she advised) without theological or seminary training.

Further, she said I should be content in knowing I had a husband in the will of the Lord and as good looking as he. She said he could have any woman he wanted. She began to schedule leadership meetings three times per week around dinner time so that by the time he got home he'd already eaten. And even after he left and arrived home within moments of his arrival they would call to pray over the phone for what seemed like hours.

There was a leak in her ministry. One service she shared a story of a family that left her ministry and shortly after was in a terrible automobile accident. She said it happened because they left her covering, and God rendered judgment. Well a couple of the women in her church were not feeling this interpretation of events. Nor were they pleased with the focus and rapid motivation of the one and only man in the ministry, my husband. They were disturbed that dinner was only available to him and there was never any for the rest of them, so they began to whisper. One of the uttered secrets was that there was a plan to pretend I was demon possessed and throw me out of her front door collectively. Another secret is that I did not cook for my husband nor did I meet his needs as a prayer partner, more specifically she said the Lord Himself revealed this to her and showed her that sexually I refused him, causing him to fast and pray frequently for strength. She even accused me of witchcraft. This, I discovered, is why the others were unfriendly towards me and would avoid me. Children of the gospel, here is a ready word! What does not come out in the wash will come out in the rinse.

I was so wounded, so broken, so disturbed; I did not know what to do, so I got on the phone with former leadership for counsel. This is the right start but we can't depend on others to pray us through, not constantly anyway. To no surprise, my husband and I wound up separated. The Pastor took him in on the second floor of her two-family home and was overjoyed. Not once did she offer to discuss reconciliation, or call me to see if I was okay. When she would see me, she had a newness of joy that words could not express. I realize now that the enemy was celebrating victory in my hour of pain. He returned, and told me that before he left he discovered that she had poured fresh garlic under his bed. He'd been informed that she was operating in witchcraft, and admitted that she had a strong lust spirit for him.

Though he had come home, things were not the same; he was very different and did not trust me. The members started coming to our home, holding meetings in our living room. I wanted it to stop, but my warning of discontent was addressed as rebellion and once again we separated. I moved out of that particular house. Our marriage was under attack, and it was absolutely not a fair fight. We are wise to realize that we wrestle not against flesh and blood, one another, but against principalities, against powers and against rulers of the darkness of this world and spiritual wickedness in high places, against the forces of evil, those who Satan uses to bring us down. [Ephesians 6:12] Let us not underestimate these powerful forces just because we can't see them.

These women were determined to destroy the possibility of reconciliation. Satan hates marriage and he hates for you to find your purpose and walk in your calling, especially with your soulmate. "Therefore, from now on, we regard no one from a worldly point of view." [2 Corinthians 5:14-16] These women and their worldy point of view were victims without realizing it: they were being used of the enemy. The enemy will use anyone and anything to have his way in your life. You see these puppets had taken matters into their own selfish interest in hopes to satisfy their burning flesh, but realistically they were operative vessels working in harmony with Lucifer himself. We have the option to choose righteousness over unrighteousness according to our own free will. Let me also confess that neither my husband nor I were exempt from error during this process. In this case we were upset with one another, disappointed in our actions and reactions which kept driving us further and further apart. If you know like I know, there is nothing to hard for God "too hard" to mend and breathe life into. Through the love of the Lord, we were able to settle our differences. God absolutely got the glory. That's how our marriage survived. When I moved, my husband realized that such discontent was not in God's plan. After all, your first ministry is your family. And so, both humbled, we decided to try for a fresh start. We forgot about what went wrong, pressing forward for the greater good.

Consider Job who was absolutely in the midst of spiritual warfare, Job was on Satan's hit list. He didn't know what befell him—he was in a whirlwind of attacks. Through all his pain and suffering, Job never lost his faith in God, and God never let Job go. When you find yourself under a series of attacks, it is indicative of spiritual warfare and probably because of some undiscovered greatness in you that is about to be made manifest in your life. Spiritual abuse is tough to overcome. It is one of the most violent attacks of them all and usually births a contrite heart. A broken spirit is not mended by a doctor, a pastor, a spouse, a close friend. While they can be vital contributors to the process, ultimately only God can heal your spirit. During such a season it is important to keep the faith and keep praying. Remember the battle is not yours; it's the Lords. You will come out of the fiery furnace as pure gold.

You will find that you get greater results, when you learn to face the music of your life and turn to God for resolve. Sometimes, for example, when my son acts up, his dad puts him on time out. My son then comes to me, appealing to my soft side, and I in turn go to my husband to reason with him. This serves to annoy my husband, who digs in his heels and refuses to change the punishment. However, I have noticed that when Silva goes to his daddy directly with a sincere heart and those big beautiful compelling eyes, his Dad embraces him and grants his request. It can be difficult to trust that someone has learned from error when you can't look into the spirit, which truly speaks. God wants us to come to him with all sincerity and total surrender concerning our life. By doing so, He can pick us up, dust us off and stretch out His loving arms to cover us.

> *Therefore put on the full armor of God, so that when the day of evil comes, you may be able to stand your ground, and after you have done everything, to stand. 14 Stand firm then, with the belt of truth buckled around your waist, with the breastplate of righteousness in place, 15 and with your feet fitted with the readiness that comes from the gospel of peace. 16 In addition to all this, take up the shield of faith, with which you can extinguish all the flaming arrows of the evil one. 17 Take the helmet of salvation and the sword of the Spirit, which is the word of God. 18 And pray in the Spirit on all occasions with all kinds of prayers and requests. With this in mind, be alert and always keep on praying for all the saints.* [Ephesians 6:13-18]

The day of evil comes in many different forms. This is why we must stay prayed up, centered and anchored in Christ Jesus—whom by the way is the only way to enter into the kingdom. God calls us to obedience, humility, ministry and perfect love. We have a duty to seek Him and resist evil. He does not ask us to go toe to toe with the devil. God is handling the battle for us. We are to resist evil by standing firm with truth, righteousness, fitted feet, faith, salvation and the spirit indwelling. We should not partake in things that detest the God we serve. We should not walk in the counsel of evil men. Further we should not mislead our brothers and sisters, making ourselves blood guilty.

Envy can lead you to the road of self-destruction. Envy and jealousy can make you consciously and unconsciously speak death concerning others. This is a dangerous emotion. Even leaders, teachers, students and followers—everyone, in fact, is at risk to operate in the spirit of envy. I have been personally attacked, because someone wanted my job, my husband, my voice, my clothes, my gifts, my children, my favor... How many times have we wanted something that someone else had? It is easy to fall into the desire to be like others, but how far will we take it? Will we sabotage them for power, position or people? What God has for you is for you. If we could stop focusing on others, we might discover the greatness set aside for us.

> *Let the word of Christ dwell in you richly as you teach*
> *and admonish one another with all wisdom, and as you*
> *sing psalms, hymns and spiritual songs with gratitude in*
> *your hearts to God.* [Colossians 3:16]

Pray with me...

> *Father please forgive me where I have sinned against*
> *others and your word. I rebuke the spirit of envy and*
> *jealousy that may be intertwined or hidden in my mo-*
> *tives. Lord, I love you and want to live for you. I real-*
> *ize that I must love my brothers and sisters with care*
> *and purpose to speak life concerning them. I turn away*
> *from my flesh, my opinions and judgments about how*
> *things should be. Teach me how to love. It is not about*
> *me, or my way or how I feel or think because in my*
> *view, error abides, in my flesh sin resides. Lord each*

day I must repent to an unrepentant God because you are perfect with eternal glory! Teach me how to diligently seek and worship you so that beyond this, the manifestation of your spirit and your light is evidenced in my behavior and in the way I interact with and speak over others. I don't want to just read the bible, praying and chanting like the Pharisees and Sadducees. I don't want to praise and worship while plotting against my brothers and sisters in Christ like a hypocrite. Lord, help me to focus on you and discover your purpose and will for my life. Lord whomever I have hurt with words, ill prayers, thoughts, speaking into or over their life, please forgive me as I send out a special healing prayer of restoration, favor, grace, mercy and new levels in you sweet Jesus. Lord I speak to the winds that they blow a triple portion of blessings on those I have wounded with my words, thoughts and prayers. Teach me how to mind my own business and shut my mouth when I am out of line. In Jesus precious name, Amen! [or] Lord, I have been wounded by people in leadership and in authority over my life. I am confused and I have secluded myself to avoid spiritual hurt, mental abuse and emotional distress. Father I don't want a hardened heart. Give me the strength to stand up, stand firm and go forward with you. Father, teach me how to forgive and how to love so that I may not block my own blessings and I can get on with my life and my destiny. Father I love you and I need you. Please usher in the Holy Spirit to mend my heart, heal my emotions and renew my mind. Lord it is fear that has me bound and I release it to you now Lord. Please dress me with power, love and stability as I journey with you.

Amen

CHAPTER 7

Insight

In gathering the value out of the storms in my life, I am encouraged because while these storms all seemed to be bigger than me and bigger than anything I thought I could survive, they were not bigger than the God I serve. Through it all God has never forsaken me. I have comfort in knowing that His word is true and He can't lie. Because He is a God of Truth, He is not bound nor His word! Even when I can't go on, I can go on, because God goes before me and covers and protects me, guarding me. I can do all things through Christ who is my strength and redeemer. Read this and anticipate a break through. I pray your strength in the Lord.

Many corporations pride themselves in work-and family-balance because they understand that balance brings about greater productivity and performance. They have realized that when external forces are compromised, the performance suffers a decline. There is an increase in disability claims, leaves of absences, low morale, and even a stress in their ability to retain talent. Remember, "Therefore, from now on, we regard no one from a worldly point of view." [2 Corinthians 5:16] As difficult as it may be to excuse others with a worldly perspective, we have to use our spiritual lenses to recognize that behind the unreasoning of others lies discontent, discord, hurt, pain, disappointment and often fear. These factors certainly cloud judgment and compromise behaviors. Where there is no balance there resides vulnerability. God explains in Ecclesiastes that we should find balance and outright says that he hates extremes:

> *Do not be over righteous, neither be over wise, why destroy yourself? Do not be over wicked, and do not be a fool, why die before your time? It is good to grasp the one and not let go of the other. The man who fears God will avoid all extremes.* [Ecclesiastes 7:16-18]

When people get on our nerves, it's second nature to get upset or impatient with them, a little tired of them, and eventually desiring to take matters into our on hands (which by the way is out of God's hands.) Can you imagine if everyone allowed their nature to rise up and take over? It's hard when you have to submit to unbalanced authority, but that is why we pray rather than prey, why we keep marching forth in the spirit of excellence.

In order to be an effective Christian we need to find balance so that we are reachable, and we can reach others as well. If we get too deep concerning any one thing we will push others away and we will miss out on the beauty of life right now. So as you live for God who created all, live a balanced life because God is balanced and requires the same of each of us.

God has not authorized the spirit of fear but of love, power and a sound mind. This word is true and is applicable across the board. It is fear that keeps us from growing and going where God has called us. It is fear that makes us double-minded. God is not the author of confusion—what God is saying is "Make up your minds. Make a decision!", rather right or wrong. Find yourself, your place, your way, and stand. If it's a job, a courtship, a business decision, going to school or to a church, whatever it is pray about it, make up your mind and stand. Don't go back-and-forth wasting time and energy in the spirit of confusion. If you can walk away from fear by deciding that it can't be a ruler in your life, you will gain more power, discover more love, and begin to make sound decisions concerning your life in Christ as a balanced and effective epistle.

> *Eye hath not seen, nor ear heard, neither have entered into the heart of man, the things which God hath prepared for them that love him. The inheritance which God has prepared for you cannot even be conceived by the natural mind of man…but God does reveal it to us "by His Spirit."* I Corinthians 2:9-10]

Anguish transcends to self doubt, self pity, insecurity, attitude, ingratitude, sickness, illness, disease, a rotten spirit, lack of energy, lack of will, lack of faith, everything stagnant and restricting. If he the adversary knows that he can immobilize you through fear, then he has the victory over your life. Perhaps you have heard many leaders preach the message that Satan comes to steal, kill, and destroy and it is through fear that he will begin to monopolize the lives of those who have fallen prey. We have to be watchful as well because this can take root in small doses in any area of your life. You will note that once you are made to feel unconfident, you no longer have the zest to perform at peak. In the absence of confidence your precision is off. Confidence is not something that bares fruit in the natural because that would be conceit. But when your spirit is strong and your strength renewed, things flow in the natural because that is the excellence of Christ granting you the grace and anointing to perform at peak. For example you may be very good at doing something and the more confirmation you get in this area the higher you go. However if you error too many times and miss you may begin to lack the same confidence in your physical skill. With that said it is not the physical evidence that make the gift special, rather the spiritual anointing and blessed assurance of knowing without a doubt that you can do something through Christ indwelling. We must be sure to give Him the glory for teaching our hands to war (get things done).

Take back what the enemy has bound and learn to loose your blessings. Speak it, believe it, anticipate it and thank God for this in advance. Great is thy faithfulness. Recognize how both life and death are in the power of the tongue. Knowing this, which will you speak over your life and over the lives of your loved ones. Beloved use your power to speak Life.

God is readying us. He is strengthening us and to whom much is given, much is required. I say to you who may have a habit in fear: God gives you talents and develops you so that you may use them mightily. Together with God there is no limit in what you can do and where you can go and how many you can touch, deliver and set free. The test is the storm. God has taught me how to just stand in the midst, but in faith!

Sing with me…

What do you do when you've done all you can and it

seems like it's never enough? And what do you say when your friends turn away, you're all alone? Tell me, what do you give when you've given your all, and it seems like you can't make it through?

Sing with me...

Stand and be sure, be not entangled in the bondage again. You just stand and be sure. God has a purpose. Yes, God has a plan.

Tell me what do you do when you've done all you can and it seems like you can't make it through. Child you just stand, you just stand, stand. Don't give up. Through the storm, through the rain, through the hurt, through the pain.

Tell me, how do you handle the guilt of your past? Tell me, how do you deal with the shame? And how can you smile when your heart is broken and filled with pain? Tell me what do you give when you've given your all seems like you can't make it through.

Don't you bow, don't bend Don't give up , don't give in Hold on , just be strong. God will step in and it won't be long After you've done all you can. After you've gone through the hurt, After you've gone through the pain. After you've gone through the storm, After you've gone through the rain. Prayed and cried, when there's nothing left to do, You just stand, Watch the Lord see you through. Yes, after you've done all you can, You just stand.

—Reverand Donnie McClurkin

CHAPTER 8

For You

I HAVE PROVIDED WORDS TO MEDITATE UPON
AND A JOURNAL TO RECORD YOUR PERSONAL EXPERIENCES.

EXERCISE

Take a moment to visualize the storms you have gone through or are going through. Close your eyes and breathe deeply. Recognize your breath as life and as spirit. Recognize that the spirit of the only true and living God indwells inside of you. Begin to inhale faith and exhale doubt and fear, inhale that which is good and clean and pure and exhale darkness, deceit and disaster. Free yourself so that flesh submits to the spirit that has been given to direct you and protect you. Visualize one storm at a time. Allow the storm to rage large in the moment; and with each exhale blow out the fire and the smoke from the storm. Begin to reduce the storm in capacity and in vigor until you reduce it to nothing. Allow all the peace and the joy of the Lord to enter each time you inhale. Meditate on His Word holding to the Promises of God. Accept the triumph! Become victorious over fear concerning the valley experiences in your life. To be free in Christ is to be free indeed!

Write down the storms and then cross them out. Write down your dreams and your purpose and highlight them with a florescent marker. Find the brightest, most beautiful marker you can get your hands on to do this. Next, give this over to God who is ultimately in control of your life. We all have storms and challenges but we must not allow them to consume us.

List your storms and then cross them out here:

_____

_____

_____

_____

_____

_____

_____

_____

_____

_____

_____

_____

_____

_____

_____

_____

_____

_____

_____

_____

Let's begin to magnify our dreams and our purpose as they align for our good. Let's focus on where we are going, as oppose to where we've come from. God makes all things beautiful in His time.

List your dreams and purpose and then highlight them here:

_____

_____

FEAR IS NOT MY BOSS

_____

_____

_____

_____

_____

_____

_____

_____

_____

_____

_____

_____

_____

_____

_____

_____

_____

_____

_____

_____

_____

_____:_____

_____

For You

PART II:
Fear

CHAPTER 9

The Spirit of Fear

Fear, like many other strongholds, is a spirit. It operates in the mind of man and is one of Satan's primary tactics dispatched to blot out faith. Without faith it is impossible to please God. Through fear, you get separated from your destiny. By no means are you or have you been created to fail. The adversary takes pleasure in seeing us stumble and fall. In fact it is his goal to cripple God's children, particularly worshippers. This is why whenever you begin to worship, the enemy of your soul launches his attack. He uses fear and he uses your area of weakness to trick and trap you, so that you are distracted enough to walk away from worshipping God, from whom all blessings flow. Your faith must continue to grow and your hope must increase. God says, "I pray that your Faith fail not." God has given us instruction in life in His word and He has gifted us with the Holy Spirit, which provides divine guidance and direction. We ought to be wise to exercise our Faith to its limitless potential. In John 8: 31-32 God imparts direction in advising, "If you hold to my teaching, you are my disciples. Then you will know the truth, and the truth will set you free." *We are all called for something!* Friend of mine, fear is a serious stronghold and undoubtedly the origin of derailed brilliance, from the point of conception. *It's an emotional precinct that stands between you and what's yours.* In other words, when you are gifted with something, Satan despises you and the gift. When you discover the gift, he sends thwarting distractions to separate you from what you must do. Shake these unclean spirits and keep it moving.

Don't take another fearful step! You have a right to freedom from all strongholds, including freedom of fear. You were born to inhabit the earth and the fullness thereof. You are a child of the Most-High God and with God before you, you can do anything but fail. Let His light so shine in you, as you journey to perfection. We are all created with purpose and a chartered plan. Therefore if we are "sent" to do something, clearly we are capable, called and built with the talent, and hardware to get it done. Fear hinders our thoughts, our execution, and ultimately our performance. Fear alters us holistically, thereby impeding our abilities to function at peak from every aspect. Fear can diminish the strength of the swift and mighty, it can rob the brilliant of intellect and bring the greatest of leaders to rapid demise. Fear is nothing to play with, and it must be checked.

From a physical perspective, fear is not an abnormal emotion, rather an internal defense mechanism triggered by a signal from the brain that releases the adrenaline that will shape our reaction to a potential threat. There are real threats and imagined threats resulting from ones individual perception toward anticipated harm. In the instance of danger fear proves useful as it fuels and prepares us for action or reaction to imposed danger. Rather real or imagined, fear is something we must face and about face in order to move on in life.

Don't take it personally.

Many people use fear to manipulate and control others, because they understand that fear is a tactic of mental warfare. When fear runs rampant in our mind it occupies much of our time and space, leaving no grounds for more nurturing seeds to grow. It is imperative to focus on breath when dealing with fear. After every challenge, you can be confident that:

You were breathing through the storm.

You are still breathing after the storm.

God is not finished with you yet!

Even in the event that you have experienced or witnessed unexplainable trauma that words could never share, please allow your spirit to receive God's miraculous healing and peace. Ask for it and anticipate it. You can and will be cleansed of past hurts and made perfectly strong. There has never been a storm that He could not calm. There has never been anything impossible for God to accomplish. Rather past, present, or future fears taunt you, do yourself a favor and give them over to God. "My people suffer for lack of knowledge" [Hosea 4:6]. some perish... So why not study to show thy-self approved! Simply knock and the door shall be opened!

We are confronting *the spirit of Fear* outside of God's intent and how it is used to keep us down trodden and broken....

The Spirit of Fear creates gaps that separate us from happiness, success, health, vitality and beyond! Sometimes you may think, *I can see it, but I just can't reach it....* Well that's just glass, baby—break it down! *What should we ask for?* Clearly and reasonably, "a teachable spirit", where balance is key! We can hear many things, but the most fruitful experience is better partnered when we heed that which we hear. There are so many interpretations of God's Word, as human nature derives our thinking. We must walk in truth and the simple truth is His ways are above our ways and His thinking above our thinking. So in the meantime we must learn to apply the aerobics of Faith, so that when Fear rears its ugly head against us, we have a means for escape. God has not forsaken us: "Lo, I am with you always, even unto the end of the world." [Matthew 28:20]

This is what we must rehearse in our hearts, our minds, and our bodies. There is no denying that experiences, obstacles and uncomfortable events will visit us as we journey to perfection, but we are better fit for the coarse when we walk in serenity accepting the things we cannot change, and when we are courageous enough to change that which we can, while exercising knowledge that births the wisdom to know the difference. Now that translates to balance, if you ask me.

The Bride of Fear courts her companion moving thru life in helpless turmoil. She embraces Fear despite its painful scorn that alienates her from her purpose, her person and her passion. She is married to Fear and committed to Pain. The Bride of Fear partakes in consummating her relationship, avoiding her inner strength, dodging her anointing.

Each time you walk away from the plan you say "I do" to fear over and over again. Free yourself!

> *There was famine in the land and the Lord appeared to Isaac and said: 'Dwell in this land, and I will be with you and bless you and perform the oath which I swore to Abraham your father.' So Isaac sowed in that land, and reaped in the same year a hundred-fold; and the Lord blessed him. So he began to prosper, and continued prospering until he became very prosperous.* [Genesis 26:1-3, 12, 13]

CHAPTER 10

The Face of Fear

Fear is the big bad wolf; don't let it be the boss of you! Don't allow the gruesome face of fear to derail your purpose, don't let it bully you into the pit, don't allow it to engulf you and scar you and deprive you of everything that is beautiful for you and your sanctified destiny. Stand up and confidently wear your glorious crown, for ye are kings and queens of great nations. We have been armed through the Word and the Word is bigger and stronger than Fear. Greater is He that is in me than he that is in the world. God means what He says, when He said "Greater." Greater is He that is in you than he that is in the world. Learn to protect yourself from yourself and anyone or anything else that operates against your Victory here and forever. Fear Not…Fear Not…Fear **NOT**…Fear **NOT**…Fear **NOT**…Fear **NOT!**

Imagine that you are walking home one dark, cold night. The streets are silent and bare. As you pass dark alleyways a chill arises, you get an airy feeling as you proceed. Where do you think that airy feeling comes from? You're gut? No. God has given you a special gift referred to as intuition. It is that quiet whisper or sometimes, loud tug in your spirit that guides you away from danger. So, walking down a street, you recognize the vulnerable atmosphere. Your instinctive wisdom gives birth to potential danger. You begin to look behind and around as you increase your stride. At this time a cat, darts out of no where, taking you by complete surprise and suddenly your muscles become tense, your heart, begins to race, your breathing increases, your eyes widen in terror, your palms sweat. You pull yourself together and proceed when suddenly, you think you've seen a shadowy figure behind a tree. You second-guess your God-given instinct but as you get closer, you proceed with caution as anticipation heightens. This fear (stimuli) begins the process for protection by sending a signal to the brain in the form of stress, fear, and or anxiety which produces a chemical release that readies us for what we know as the "Fight-or-Flight Syndrome." What will you do in this instance? Will you take flight or prepare to fight at the face of danger? Hard to tell, since fear is an autonomic response, we can't really predict our physical behaviors and performance when danger strikes.

GET WISDOM AND KNOWLEDGE BUT IN ALL YOUR GETTING, GET UNDERSTANDING. [PROVERBS 4:5-7]

Fear takes place in the unconscious mind, as fear is not something that happens consciously. If fear takes place unconsciously, then it is pretty safe to say that you can meet and manage fear by strengthening your core. Your core would be your spirit. Everything we are and everything we do is directly linked to our core or our spirit man, which means, that it can be managed as we strengthen our spirit man. How does the spirit man acquire strength? You become strong by fasting, by prayer and supplication. *"He desires to abide in the praises of His people."* There is absolute power in worship and praise But before we go there, let us get wisdom and knowledge about the physical progression, so that we can understand the importance of the spiritual growth and empowerment, we'll need to manage emotional turmoil.

The emotional process of creating fear begins with a scare stimulus and ends with the fight-or-flight response. Let me provide some insight around the natural process concerning fear as an emotional activity.

Thalamus:

> In your brain, the Thalamus dictates where to send incoming details that enters via sight, hearing, taste, and finally touch. Ok that's your five senses.

Sensory Cortex:

> The Sensory Cortex interprets the detail received from your five senses.

Hippocampus:

> The Hippocampus manages the essence of your consciousness and recalls these experiences.

Amygdala:

> The Amygdala decodes emotions, determines possible threat, stores fear memories.

Hypothalamus:

> The "fight or flight" response is activated through the Hypothalamus.

Traditional psychoanalysis assumes that the course taken by mental events is autonomically regulated by the pleasure principle. Fair enough! We can follow and grasp the physical process behind fear, but we cannot address the root unless we embrace the truth in the supernatural realm. It is evidenced that we tend to make decisions that appease pleasure, stroke egos, and avoid pain. "Put to death what is earthly in you, fornication, impurity, passion, evil desire and covetousness, which is idolatry." [Colossians 3:5]

The issue here is we are in pursuit of what pleases us rather than what pleases God. What we seek for pleasure will only leave us empty and yearning always, for more. The stroking of our flesh and our egos leads to self-righteousness. We wind up in debt, in sickness, in isolation. "For if you live according to the flesh (the sinful nature) you will die, but it by the Spirit you put to death the deed of the body you will live." [Romans 8:13] Pleasure can be a spiritual battle grounds. For we wrestle not against flesh and blood, but against principalities, against powers, against the rulers of the darkness of this world, against spiritual wickedness in high places.

> *In order that the just requirement of the law might be fulfilled in us, who walk not according to the flesh but according to the Spirit. For those who live according to the flesh set their minds on the things of the flesh, but those who live according to the Spirit set their minds on the things of the Spirit. To set the mind on the flesh is death, but to set the*

mind on the Spirit is life and peace. For the mind that is set on the flesh is hostile to God; it does not submit to God's law, indeed it cannot; and those who are in the flesh cannot please God. But you are not in the flesh; you are in the Spirit, if in fact the Spirit of God dwells in you. Any one who does not have the Spirit of Christ does not belong to him. But if Christ is in you, although your bodies are dead because of sin, your spirits are alive because of righteousness. If the Spirit of him who raised Jesus from the dead dwells in you, he who raised Christ Jesus from the dead will give life to your mortal bodies also through his Spirit which dwells in you. So then, brethren, we are debtors, not to the flesh, to live according to the flesh-- for if you live according to the flesh you will die, but if by the Spirit you put to death the deeds of the body you will live. For all who are led by the Spirit of God are sons of God. [Romans 7: 4-17]

While we understand that fear is a physical response to potential danger and a God given instrument that is designed to protect us, we must also submit our flesh (our thinking) to the spirit (our walk) so that it does not over take us and rob us of the balance necessary to operate in this realm in a healthy manner. Mild fear is beneficial because it keeps us from foolish danger, such as walking into a ball of fire, walking off a ship in the middle of an ocean, walking in front of on coming traffic, or off of a cliff.

Fear has many expressions; fear, dread, fright, alarm, panic, terror, trepidation:

Fear is a painful agitation in the presence or anticipation of danger. The most general term and implies anxiety and or loss of courage.

Fright implies the shock of sudden, startling fear.

Fright implies awareness of immediate danger.

Panic implies unreasoning and overmastering fear causing hysterical activity; Terror implies the most extreme degree of fear.

Trepidation adds to dread the implications of timidity, trembling and hesitation.

—Merriam Webster Online Collegiate Dictionary

Fear is the inability to tap into the power within; it immobilizes its victim, thereby creating gates that encage the free gift of life. These invisible boundaries are the platform of spiritual control. They take complete advantage of the feeble and wretched by treading upon your courage and adulterating your Faith. Ask for guidance: "Lord show me how you would have me to pray, order my words and guard them dear Lord." Pray for a teachable spirit. *"Lord please grant me a teachable spirit, that I may heed Your Word, Your Will and Your Way and properly discern it for the value and fruit of my life—as a worthy epistle seen and read of all men"*

Now there is that word "all" again; clearly *all* men are witnessing your life, those that are both good and bad. There are those that are routing for you, and those who are against you. Remember, remember, and remember Fear is a spirit that creeps in through possessions, resources, and energy in its abundance or the lack thereof. So learn to exercise faith over fear. I got to a place in my life where I got tired of being tired. It all seemed so complicated, but I discovered that this was not my battle after all. Suddenly I had a simple epiphany: *You know what fear? You are not the boss of me!* I will not allow you to plant seeds of sickness, failure, inability, inadequacy, unworthiness… I will not rehearse lies in my thoughts any more. I am taking your shackles off my feet so I can prance! STRONG MAN, get out of my house, get away from my family, my career, my walk, my purpose, my dreams, "my" Faith, spirit, mind and body, GET OUT! I made up my mind, I armored my spirit and I proclaim that *Fear is Not MY Boss!* I have the authority to speak change:

Fear **NOT**…Fear **NOT**…Fear **NOT!**

CHAPTER 11

The Origin of Fear

"FEAR IS THAT LITTLE DARK ROOM WHERE NEGATIVES ARE DEVELOPED." —MICHAEL PRITCHARD

Negative emotions result in serious consequences. You can become insecure, paranoid and immobilized. Your judgment can become clouded, creating the inability to trust others. Negative emotions can manifest into thoughts or acts of violence. It can make you a doubter instead of a believer. We are composed of mind, body, and spirit—our fears can abide mentally, physically and spiritually. We cannot exist in body without spirit. When the spirit is broken or the psyche is threatened, all factors are compromised.

Healthy fear triggered by the threat of danger can be a healthy line of defense. For example: if you trip, you use your hands to break the fall. Your brain's fear of injury sends the signal to your body to protect itself from injury. But this type of fear is not dangerous. What is dangerous is the kind of fear that grips our spirit man and perverts our psychological well-being in situations that are both real and imagined.

Fear comes from many places. We become fearful; I say "become" because we were not born in fear. It is a result of what you've seen, heard, experienced, or witnessed at some point in your life. When we are born we are fearless, trusting and dependent upon love and love alone. In spirit we trust God and the power of His perfection and unfailing love, we do not fear because we know not fear. We simply proceed in faith and in love, and when we do this our spirit is sound.

As we grow we learn about the things that hurt, endanger, and threaten us. With this learned knowledge and experience, we develop either normal fear or dangerous fear that leads us to isolation in a very distant place. So we either build ourselves or we build our fears. Many fear death, storms, illness, confinement, heights, flying, people, social situations, snakes, rats, mice, worms, spiders, nature you name it. The spirit of fear is a natural emotion, but when it makes us phobic, when our anxieties are so strong that we alter our lives to accommodate it, it becomes a problem. I call it a devouring bully. This can change our entire physical, mental and spiritual makeup drastically, rapidly and dangerously. In the presence of this kind of fear, the thought of joy, happiness and peace are not injected. When fear is eradicated, life begins!

Fear is evident when you feel tension, anxiety, stress, dread, fright, terror, alarm, panic, etc. You will also notice in the presence of fear, some very real physical symptoms that take place:

shortness of breath, palpitation, light headedness, feeling of faint, hot and cold flashes, numbness, trembling and shaking, chest pain, headaches, and the inability to focus. These feelings happen regardless of whether the fear is real or imaginary. The mind is a powerful instrument that can play an entire orchestrated composition only to find the ensemble never really existed at all. Fear can paint a picture that seems real but is not. Think back on an event where you thought you saw something approaching that turned out to be a shadow or a piece of fabric. Were you not instantly engulfed with the symptoms of fear as you perceived an imaginary threat?

There are endless possibilities in the essence and beauty of now. What happened yesterday and what may happen tomorrow does not have to dictate the present If you allow the truth of freedom to reign, then the gates of yesterday and the doubts for tomorrow will have to take a back seat to the now.

God has provided so many opportunities for us. Do not wait until the eleventh hour to address the area of approaching disaster. I can never understand why most people wait until it's almost, if not too late. We wait until we are stricken with illness before we eat right, exercise and pray. Then we run for the quick fix. Why not be in the spirit so that we are fit for the test? In life we can be certain that while on the potter's wheel, discomfort will take place, while in the fiery furnace, things will get hot, while in the midst of a storm we will be tossed and turned.

I once read a story about some of the world's worst interviews. In one particular interview, the subject had been answering a series of questions and felt panic coming on. He asked if he could be excused so that he could talk to his counselor for a moment. He began a breathing exercise and calmly whipped out his cellular phone to contact his psychiatrist in the midst of his interview. The subject was so crippled by insecurity, in the eleventh hour, he couldn't make it through an interview without crumbling. Absolutely, counseling is effective and clearly has its benefits, but we have to discover that "He" that is in me is far greater than he that is in the world. Don't view the crutch as the source. The crutch is the crutch. The SOURCE is the SOURCE! I am for counseling, don't misunderstand me, I feel that medicine has it's place also, but who are you and what in the world can you do if you empty your storage to man. So if you are at the point of threatening danger what form of treatment will be available and prove sufficient in time to pull you through?

"My Grace is Sufficient for thee; for My strength is made perfect in your weakness." [2 Corinthians 12:9] When we have divine trust, temperance, and active faith we become spiritually wise and emotionally rich. In the freedom of abundant living we are empowered to stand in the storm, walk through the flood, and fight through the fire. Fighting with faith shielded, guarded, protected and armored with the breastplate of righteousness. Understand that more important than fearing the change that the storm may bring is the wonderful change that God will birth in you and render when you surrender to him and lay your every burden down.

Stand therefore having girded your waist with truth; Stand therefore, having your loins girt about with truth, and having on the breastplate of righteousness; And your feet shod with the preparation of the gospel of peace; Above all, taking the shield of faith, wherewith ye shall be able to quench all the fiery darts of the wicked. And take the helmet of salvation, and the sword of the Spirit,

140

which is the word of God. [Ephesians 6:14-17]

Dark and light cannot co-exist in the same space. Whenever light is present in darkness it reigns supreme. When dark attempts its presence in light, it dissipates. Then there is the extreme perception of fear that invites phobic states. A fire phobia, for example, assumes that any degree of fire cannot be contained and disaster will fall regardless of the forum. I may find it beautiful to stand on a mountain top and spend hours inhaling its glory. Another may wind up in a serious state of anxiety, wanting to vomit as he looks down from such a high point. When unease becomes fear and fear becomes terror, it has spiraled out of control, creating invisible gates that keep us bound in life through irrational thoughts, chronic panic and anxiety.

CHAPTER 12

The Scars of Fear

The scars of fear can be found in the people who are sent to echo your yester sins. These individuals are sent to keep you in the mindset of your past, so that you are too confused to focus on who you are in Christ. Often it is those who are closest to you who are the reminders; because they know enough to throw the jabs that hurt most. They tend to be in worse shape than they would like to make you think you are. Don't bother to question a thing, just resist them and march. They will flee. You see, their very life force is directly linked to the celebration in your demise. They flee because they are drained and worn out by your ability to resist them. You can't play with Satan's puppets. Let God be God. Focus on your relationship with the Prince of Peace.

God created you beautifully, fearlessly and wonderfully, powerfully yet tenderly. He selected you, gifted you and set you apart for His intended purpose. He then crowned you with both humility and honor of royal priesthood. The blood of Christ is with you. You are the flavor of God and you have the favor of God. The enemy can't stand it. The sweet essence of Christ on you is plain bothersome to the enemy. It makes him sick, so he wants to degrade you, rape you, accuse you, and he tries to do it all in the likeness of Jesus. He is the prince of darkness and he hates light. Because you are blessed, it is your light he is after.

Good news! You can do all things through Christ your strength and savior! You can keep your job, your spouse, your children, your house, your health, your confidence and your safety. What door God opens, no man can shut. Having the favor of God is sweet. His Grace surely is sufficient and His mercy endures forever. You were born to be victorious. You did not land here by accident, and by no means are you a mistake.

Everyone knows that faith without works is dead, and that which you sow you will reap. If you sow much and work hard, you will be rewarded greatly. Once you are on course concerning your destiny, darts from every direction will aim for bulls-eye. Let this be a sign that greatness is about to be birthed in you, so keep pushing onward. You are probably closer to your purpose than you know. Don't allow guilt to make you walk away from lifetime opportunities and your treasures.

You may find during difficult times that envy against you will arise. The nature of a man is to climb higher than others, so when God is blessing you, when you are performing in excellence, folk become conniving. In the same breath, when you see the blessed season for someone else don't allow jealousy to use you to speak negative words against the one who is winning. Join them in the celebration of their victory. Encourage others and build them up along the way. Soon your day will come and you will want to share your joy. God created us to worship Him and to delight in one another. He knew we would need one another to learn, build and grow. Fellowship is so important to the ministry which is your life. God is a God of order, decency, and planning. We must strive to be like him to maintain a healthy approach in all that we do. "Group think" has been discovered to produce greater results than the old system or hierarchy approach. Avoid the spirit of division—you were born to win souls and in an empty hall, no one gets the prize.

One of the worst things in the world is to see the beauty of your neighbor operating in the power of his gifts as you try to smuggle them. Find yourself in yourself, not in someone else. Just because your brother is a doctor, doesn't mean you should be one. The whole time we are coveting our neighbors' gifts, we may be traveling opposite God's will for our life. Find yourself in God!

Be patient with yourself and your process: Rome wasn't built in a day. When you move too quickly, you burn out. Frustration can lead to mistakes that have penalties attached, allowing the enemy to corrode your thinking and reasoning. Do all things in decency and in order. Don't rush into relationship and agreements, use wisdom. Don't compromise your integrity or your morals. Know your Father's Voice.

When you surrender to God and accept him as your Lord and Savior, you become a new creature in Him. You will learn this and come to embrace this truth. The enemy dwells in the "remember when's". If you have a good report card, it is difficult to blemish your state of renewal. What God washes is clean indeed and the enemy knows this. So he will be masterful at attempting to remind you of your faults. The whole plan is to destroy you, sift you as wheat and keep you away from the land of milk and honey. He will even have you to replay the old days, in your mind you rewind. Be smart, be strong, and recognize the fruit of the messenger.

Guilty blood is on the hands of the man that scatter God' sheep: don't turn people away from the word with a negative attitude. Find your area of expertise, and go forth in the spirit of excellence. Be wise, be gentle and find balance. God wants wisdom and order and love in the mix. We can't just do it our way—we must live in the world, and make room for God in our world. So if you sing for a living—sing cleanly. If you dance for a living—do it modestly. If you use make-up or have a job in cosmetics—do your job honestly, and know that makeup doesn't make you any more or less holy. In Romans Chapter 4, God reminds us that whatever you do, do it unto Him.

Don't allow people to attack your livelihood when you know and God knows your heart. That is why you better seek Him and get to know Him for yourself. I have seen too many souls confused by others, with the purest intentions.

Don't play the blame game

It is tough to move forward when all you do is blame others for your difficulties. Every man was given a measure of gifts and talents. Every man was called for a divine purpose. Every man has a chance to make a difference, and every man has free will. It is a miserable place when you believe that your destiny is in the hands of another man. No man can curse you, and no weapon formed against you can prosper with God before you. When you talk and walk this misery, you give it truth and power and so shall it be. "As you seek to fulfill your destiny in Christ, you will acknowledge that the area of your greatest testing will become the area of your greatest anointing."

Fear comes in many different faces, personalities, vehicles. When fear takes a seat, the intent is to move in and stay for as long as possible. Once fear takes its place it can control and defeat its victim. By studying the Word of God and spending time with others who serve Him you can learn and become equipped to recognize this spirit and check it at the door. Beyond that you will begin to apply the Word of God to your life in every aspect and in balance, giving you a conditional attitude.

Pray this way:

> *Father I humbly come to you asking that you forgive me in my error concerning your will for my life. Lord, please help me to get on track moving forward rather than backward. Please ready my heart, my mind and my spirit for my purpose. Lord, grant me a teachable spirit and crown me with wisdom and understanding. I don't want to twist your word or your will. I pray that my spirit gains strength over my physical man so that I may fully bring you honor.*

CHAPTER 13

For You II

I HAVE PROVIDED WORDS TO MEDITATE UPON
AND A JOURNAL TO RECORD YOUR PERSONAL
EXPERIENCES

EXERCISE

When we are dark and heavy and unforgiving how in the world can we move forward with so much heaviness around us? It's like trying to complete a walkathon with a million bricks tied onto your shoulders; you just can't move. Close your eyes in the name of Jesus and inhale light and exhale darkness, inhale love and exhale hate, inhale faith and exhale fear, do this until you feel a sense of peace and freedom that is rightfully yours. It is so much easier to free your self when you represent light and love and faith and so important "forgiveness."

Write down the episodes of hurt, fear and sin, then cross them out. Replace them with good thoughts and good visions for yourself and others, and highlight them with a florescent marker. Give this over to God, who is ultimately in control of your life. We all have fears and hurts but we must not allow them to consume us.

List your fears, disappointments and shackles and then
cross them out here:

_____

_____

_____

_____

_____

_____

_____

_____

_____

_____

_____

_____

For You

_____

_____

_____

_____

_____

_____

List your dreams and purpose here:

_____

_____

_____

_____

_____

_____

_____

_____

_____

_____

_____

FEAR IS NOT MY BOSS

_____

_____

_____

_____

_____

_____

_____

_____

Do not worry about food and drink

Or about the things you'll wear.

Is life not more then food and drink?

See the birds up in the air?

They do not plant or harvest,

Nor store food in the barn,

But your Heavenly Father feeds them

And keeps them safe and warm.

Look at the lovely lilies

In the meadows where they grow.

For You

They do not want for anything,

God cares for them I know.

He adorns them with such beauty

'Tis there for all to see.

Would He not go the extra mile

When it comes to you and me?

Don't worry about tomorrow;

the best is yet to be

When you invite the Heavenly Father

To come and dwell with thee.

Focus your eyes upon Jesus;

And your problems will soon grow dim;

When you go to the Father in prayer;

and cast all your burdens on Him.

Now it came to pass on a certain day, that he went into a ship with his disciples: and he said unto them, Let us go over unto the other side of the lake. And they launched forth. [Matthew 8:24]

But as they sailed he fell asleep: and there came down

a storm of wind on the lake; and they were filled with water, and were in jeopardy. [Mark 4:37]

And they came to him, and awoke him, saying, Master, Master, we perish. Then he arose, and rebuked the wind and the raging of the water: and they ceased, and there was a calm. And he said unto them, where is your faith? And they being afraid wondered, saying one to another, what manner of man is this! For he commandeth, even the winds and water, and they obey him. [Luke 8:22-25]

FEAR NOT...FOR LO, I AM WITH YOU ALWAYS.

PART III
Faith

CHAPTER 14

Surrender

THE SONG GOES SOMETHING LIKE THIS...

MY STORAGE IS EMPTY AND I AM AVAILABLE TO YOU...USE ME LORD!

Sometimes, you have to release to go forward. It's hard to move forward when you're carrying weights, parcels, and bags, it slows you down and wears you out. There is a song by Mary, Mary that says, "Take the shackles off my feet so I can dance." With shackles you could wiggle a bit, maybe bop your head to the music, but your best, most beautiful steps are restricted. God bless Aaliyah's soul, but her demise was the result of too much baggage on her flight. How can you soar with so much weight you can barely get off the ground? Upon discovering your immobility, you shake some things, but still can't soar. So you evaluate, shake more, and still can't soar. In the scheme of things you are still holding onto some areas where God wants to take control. If we would just give it to God, He would iron things out for us. He would get rid of what needs to go, refine what is rough, and protect that which is really good. You have to surrender mind body and spirit, so He can fill you with what you need to prevail.

"For I know the plans I have for you,' declares the Lord, 'plans to prosper you and not to harm you, *plans to give you hope and a future.*" [Jeremiah 29:11] Clearly God has created you with a purpose, and planted you to be victorious. He has spoken power over you and your concerns here and beyond. God will guide us step by step, but in order for us to answer the call we must first believe, accept, and follow Him in total surrender. Surrendering should not be a struggle or difficult decision. You should find peace in allowing God to rule over your life. If God had to force you in the way that you should go, how would we ever come to know, understand and trust Him? If God did not provide the option to choose, how could we choose obedience and surrender?

Delight yourself also in the Lord, and He shall give you the desires of your heart. Commit your way to the Lord, trust also in Him, and He shall bring it to pass Rest in the Lord, and wait patiently for Him. [Psalm 37:4-7]

Just as He guided Moses to deliver His people from the Egyptian hand of bondage, He is there for you. Moses, with God's help, carried the Israelites out of bondage while sharing God's intent to deliver them into the Promised Land, a land flowing with milk and honey. " 'For I know the plans I have for you,' declares the Lord, 'plans to prosper you and not to harm you, plans to give you hope and a future.'" [Jeremiah 29:11] To surrender our every care, concern, and personal will to someone, the guard must come down, and so it is with our relationship with God the Father. He will instruct you as you seek Him and learn of His ways, just as Moses did.

If you recall, many of the Israelites had great doubt, and Moses had to constantly intercede to keep them faithful. God showed them dozens of supernatural wonders, even the parting of a sea, yet they all displayed wavering faith. Eventually, God would not allow any man over the age of twenty to enter into the Promised Land as a result of their doubt. You can't just say you believe in God. That is not enough.

"He who has My commandments and keeps them, he it is who loves Me; and he who loves Me shall be loved by My Father, and I will love him, and will disclose Myself to him." [John 14:21] No one said life would be anything close to easy. There will be trials, tribulations, challenges and obstacles. There will be many afflictions on your path to righteous living, but God has declared us victorious in Him and He has promised to see us through to the end. We simply have to learn to let go and let God, by allowing Him to be the Lord over our life and the Savior of our soul. It is a non-stop daily task we have much work to do, but a task that makes sense. Why would we want to carry the burdens that life presents on our own? It's beautiful the gift of life, when we do it God's way, by abiding to His will for our life. God wants to reveal to every one of us exactly what we are called to do, by shaping us and making us to ready us for the call. The shaping process is often uncomfortable and usually difficult, in fact reminiscent of the birthing process. Imagine the intense pressure an infant feels coming through such a tight course to get here. Birthing is simply painful.

While you may have attempted to escape painful experiences in your quest to discover your purpose, it remains inevitable. You run, seeking and believing so many different doctrines and practices concerning your life in hopes to find a quick fix, a microwave miracle or an overnight sensation. When you find yourself fearing what may happen as a result of a storm, in panic you either withdraw or attack. The question is, wouldn't it be so much easier if we'd just hear God? I am so thankful that God is not emotional. God is perfect and precise. How terrific is it that He desires to use us for His Glory? He expressed that He is not looking for lukewarm servants; if He is going to use anyone, it sure won't be halfway. Imagine baking a cake for someone halfway and expecting them to eat it. Similarly, it is not wise to run from place to place gathering half the truth and half a lie. In God you will discover truth and be set free.

If we have a heart after God's own will, we are less likely to be a slave to our own ego and perceptions of self and others. We often act or judge in direct correlation to our opinions about a person or situation, and in turn we are perceived in the same manner by others. We can harm one another with our opinions and judgments as well.

With that said this is why we would be wise to come under the subjection, divine direction, love and power of the true and living God. What God does for one He will do for another according to His good and perfect will.

> John reads on this wise; *If anyone chooses to do God's will, he will find out whether my teaching comes from God or whether I speak on my own. He who speaks on his own does so to gain honor for himself, but he who works for the honor of the one who sent him is a man of*

truth; there is nothing false about him. [John 7:17-18]

We waste so much time and energy trying to make it on our own. We experience detours in our wilderness journey that we could altogether avoid by giving our life over to God.

"Free will allows you to follow the dictates of your own heart" —Cecil B. Ward

Since God gave you free will, He will allow you to figure out your own way, hoping you will come to the realization that He is there to bridge the gap. God can be your bridge over troubled waters. "I will instruct you and teach you in the way you should go; I will counsel you and watch over you." [Psalms 32:8] If you want to do it alone and face the world in and of yourself, He will lift His hand because God said "I will not always strive with man." You will grow weary from running and realize, hopefully, that as you run you are getting further from the seat of safety.

> *Come unto me all ye that labour and are heavy laden and I will give you rest; take my yoke upon you and learn of me; for my yoke is easy and my burden is light.* [Matthews 11:28-30]

Christ, said "I can of myself do nothing; the father within me he doeth the works." [John 5:19] God is the Word and His Word is true. If He be in you, thereto dwells the truth, which is the light. The truth arises from within, not from without. Let your light so shine before men that they may see your good works and glorify your Father which is in heaven. It is what's inside that counts: looking the part and going through the motions is a dangerous state. This is what happens when you accept God as your Savior but decide to rule your own life rather than allowing your Lord and Savior to complete you. You are like a half baked cake which is useless and sickening. Let's not make Him sick of us.

CHAPTER 15

Glorify

No matter what I am going through, I find refuge in the midst of praise and worship. When you truly enter into the gates of thanksgiving, you find yourself in absolute atmospheric heaven. The presence of the Lord is so powerful that you can't help but escape what was going on or going wrong in your life. God's glory is gregarious, it is grand glorious, it is breathtaking, it is magnificent. His glory is an extreme radiance and mindblowing. His glory is awesome and powerful and captivating. It is why every knee will bow and every tongue will confess that He is Lord. With the glory of God, the devil is defeated. It is His beauty, His brilliance, His amazement that reigns supreme.

Praise and worship should be offered to God who alone is worthy of all praise and honor. Praise ought to be the most sincere gesture to acknowledge, thank and exalt the most high God. God has many names and can be addressed in the most endearing expressions: for example, *Abba Father, or Dear Father* during praise and worship. Human beings are positively responsive to praise and will even go out of the way to get it. Praise energizes us and boost our self-esteem and confidence. How often we look at the tangible evidence of our works and loose sight of the one that made it all possible.

Notice how when you do something great, you want your name associated with this success in flashing lights. Look at me, look what I've done! You want everyone to know that it was you. It's perfectly natural to enjoy recognition for our good works, but we should ultimately give the honor to whom it is due, and stop robbing God of His works. It is because of Gods grace and mercy that you do what you do. It is His gifts and favor that makes it all possible for you.

There is no man on the face of this earth that will not see trial. "God said many are the afflictions of the righteous but the Lord delivers us out of them all." [Psalms 34:19] We are not to deliver ourselves, God does this for us. We just have to surrender and accept His direction. We can draw from the true substance within from the true and living God.

God first wants us to choose Him, and through this choice, we represent Him. When you represent someone, you must first learn as much about him or her as possible. Somewhat like a courtship, you go for long walks together, you have long penetrating conversations. By spending time, often quiet time, you learn about one another's mannerisms and desires. When you desire to know someone and prove your love to them, as well as be loved by them, you share things that can only be shared between the two of you. In time, you really and truly come to know your special friend for yourself. Not by hearsay, or by what you see, but by what you know first hand, up close and personal.

Coming to know God for yourself is easy, not something that should be forced or dreaded. The more you seek Him and encounter His love, the more you will discover that there is no greater love than God's love, which bares all things. Getting to know God is a great and endless experience. You will find a friend in Him that never grows weary. He is waiting for you, hoping that this day may be the day that you decide to walk with Him and trust Him with every aspect of your life. He has been gracious enough to allow you to enter into the diary of His heart, which is His true and living Word. He has been so merciful that He ushers His Holy Spirit, so that you may, through your gifts become wise and guided.

Communicating with God can take place any time and any-where, there is no form or fashion. Prayer is not something you must rehearse in order for it to be effective. Through prayer we can speak to Him in any language at any tone or pitch, even in silence. We can murmur and God clearly hears our cry. Just get Him on your mind, in your heart and on your spirit. He feels you and is connected to you. God wants us to humble ourselves to pray. Prayer is something you do best when humbled before the Lord, doing away with -isms and schisms, rehearsed lines and orchestrated words. Prayer is not something we do to get attention or gain approval from others. God can't and won't consider such attempts.

When with God it is okay to sit and chat with Him as long as you like, so long as your heart is genuine. You are safe and comfort-able, and He does not hold anything against you. It's like holding hands with your mate and stating your dreams one for another. You are not afraid because you know this person has your back. Well with God, in prayer, you can have a natural conversation and state your concerns, plainly and simply. Too often, we see others pray and want to immolate the manner in which they pray. This is relatively innocent. It is wonderful to see the zeal and desire to please God. What you have to understand is that God wants you, not somebody else. Since He is so patient and kind, He will wait for you to discover Him for yourself in your own voice.

"When a mans ways are pleasing to the Lord, He makes even his enemies live at peace with him." [Proverbs 16:7] This is not to frown upon hype (or as we call it hoop) that is real. The hype and the hoop come in time and from within. It comes when you have the word down in your belly and in your heart, on your mind and in your walk. When you seek God, read His Word, obey His commands, commit to Him, pray and pray and stand and stand, live for Him, spread the gospel, and tap into His anointing. The Anointing that dwells inwardly because of His Spirit that is in us, you somehow get a new dance and a new song even a new praise. It is what I call the "In the Know Zone." When you know that you know that you know God, it births a new man in you that you may have never been aware, existed. It will teach you to shout and bring forth those irrevocable gifts in new dimensions. It will accompany unspeakable joy and cause others to see you as peculiar. This will attract others to the Christ in you!

> If my people, who are called by my name, will humble themselves and pray and seek my face and turn from their wicked ways, then will I hear from heaven and will forgive their sin and will heal their land. [2 Chronicles 7:14]

Humility comes before honor. Go humbly before the throne of God, that he may honor your petition according to His good and perfect will for your life and others. Prayer is so very important because it changes things. If God fashioned words with power, declaring life and death in the power of the tongue, how much more power would be words driven by prayer. Prayer is a mighty tool and it will pierce the heart of man and provoke change.

Be careful not to do your 'acts of righteousness' before men, to be seen by them. If you do, you will have no reward from your Father in heaven.

So when you give to the needy, do not announce it with trumpets, as the hypocrites do in the synagogues and on the streets, to be honored by men. I tell you the truth, they have received their reward in full.

But when you give to the needy, do not let your left hand know what your right hand is doing, so that your giving may be in secret. Then your Father, who sees what is done in secret, will reward you.

And when you pray, do not be like the hypocrites, for they love to pray standing in the synagogues and on the street corners to be seen by men. I tell you the truth, they have received their reward in full.

But when you pray, go into your room, close the door and pray to your Father, who is unseen. Then your Father, who sees what is done in secret, will reward you.

And when you pray, do not keep on babbling like pagans,

for they think they will be heard because of their many words. Do not be like them, for your Father knows what you need before you ask him. [Matthew 6:1-8]

Jesus rebukes those who pray using repetitions. He wants the sweetness back in the mouths of His children. Through prayer you can address needs, concerns, lack, gratitude, thanksgiving, fear, weakness, strength, and direction. Cry out to the hills from whence cometh your help. I am so confident in His promises. I dare you to cry out. I know change will come: cry out!

Then they cried out to the Lord in their trouble, and he brought them out of their distress. He stilled the storm to a whisper; the waves of the sea were hushed. They were glad when it grew calm, and he guided them to their desired haven. [Psalm 107:28-30]

To get to know God and to please Him, we have to pray often. To increase our faith, we have to read His Word. To serve Him we must be willing to serve and do the necessary work to activate the faith based power that is inside.

Rejoice in the Lord always. I will say it again: Rejoice!

Let your gentleness be evident to all. The Lord is near.

Do not be anxious about anything, but in everything, by prayer and petition, with thanksgiving, present your requests to God.

And the peace of God, which transcends all understanding, will guard your hearts and your minds in Christ

Jesus. [Philippians 4:6-7]

When a child wants something from his parents, he goes to them in kindness to make a request. Because of the way he approaches his parents, they are humbled to hear the child and within reason grant the request, within reason. With more experience and wisdom, we will make a decision for the greater good. The child may not always understand our answer but they come to understand it as they mature. God wants us to be sensitive enough to heed His word, communicate with Him in prayer and recognize the unction of His Holy Spirit. We have His promise that the fervent prayer of a righteous man accomplishes much [Hebrews 4:15-16]. Whatever has you down can't keep you there.

"May God glorify His name in our lives as we believe in Him enough to come to Him often in prayer." [James 5:16-18] When we do pray, we ought to be careful what we ask for. That is why the model prayer guides us to say unto the Lord, "as thy will be done;" when we pray, we need to be reminded that God's will is good and perfect. We can go to him humbly, repenting daily of our transgressions and asking for anything in the name of Jesus according to His will. The door is open, but when we approach the throne of grace, we are guided to avoid stumbling blocks that may hinder our prayer life.

We can pray to be in constant communication with our Father. We can pray to spend time getting to know Him better, or we can present our petitions in prayer. God desires a true relationship with His children. For example, my daughter is a college student, with a thriving career, a social circle, and other obligations. However, in order to maintain our relationship, she makes time for me. We talk, share, and go places together. If she only came to me when she needed something. I would feel left out, perhaps taken for granted. No one wants to be loved in the name of "what can you do for me."

God does not want to receive only prayers for help—He desires a real relationship, as a parent does with a child. As a mother, it is important for me to feed my children, get them multivitamins or vaccines to protect them. Similarly, God wants to nourish the spirit man to keep you vibrant in Him. Prayer is the best way to do this. Just talk to your Father and find out as much as you can about Him. Listen quietly and you will hear His voice. He will be a lamp to your feet and a light to your path. If you take one step God will always take two.

I love to praise His name. He is holy, righteous, wonderful, beautiful, patient, kind, loving, perfect, unwavering, unfailing, devoted, consistent, thoughtful, marvelous, endearing, friendly, matchless! He is worthy, worthy, worthy, to be praised. To praise is to express adoration. To worship God is to acknowledge His sovereignty and just due. We exalt you Lord. When we sing praises, we praise God enthusiastically. It should be effortless and natural. *Abba Father You are extremely supreme!* When you look over your life and the goodness of God, you ought to be able to magnify His Holiness, establishing as true, that there is absolutely none like Him.

CHAPTER 16

Intimate Walk

"My sheep know my voice and a stranger they will not follow," says the Lord in the Gospel of John. You may ask yourself, *am I His sheep?* How do I know His voice? You must pray and ask God to reveal Himself to you and He will show you the way. It's just as simple as saying "Lord I want to know your voice. Please make sensitive, my spirit, open my ears and illuminate my eyes to your voice and your will, so that I will know the difference between the spirit of truth and the spirit of error."

"Assuredly I say to you, unless you are converted and become as little children, you will by no means enter the kingdom of heaven. Therefore who ever humbles himself as this little child, is the greatest in the Kingdom of Heaven." [Matt 18:3,4] The way into the heart of God and His kingdom is by the simple trust and dependence of a child. Jesus once said "I thank you Father Lord of heaven and earth that you have hidden these things from the wise and prudent and have revealed them to babes." [Matthew 11:25] It is better to please

God who has called you to service, than to please man.

When you hear the word, it is important that you understand the scriptures so you may be taught the mysteries of the gospel. This is why bible study at church and at home is so very important. "When anyone hears the word of the kingdom and does not understand it, then the wicked one comes and snatches away what was sown in his heart, this is he who receives seed by the waste side." [Matthew 13:19] The word, is a full coarse meal. Beyond solid teaching, the intimate walk takes place when you diligently seek a relationship with God our Father. It is independent of form or fashion. It is one on one and no one can build this intimate relationship for you.

God is looking for a unique relationship with every one of His children and you can't get there through the prayers and petitions of others. You have to earnestly and genuinely seek God for your self. When you walk intimately with the Lord, no one will have to confirm your relationship for you—you will know! "Let your heart retain my words; keep my commandments, and live." [Proverbs 4:4] Get wisdom! Seek understanding! Exalt understanding, and she will promote you; she will bring you honor, when you embrace her. She will place on your head an ornament of grace; a crown of glory she will deliver to you.

I have a good friend Charlotte, as close to me as a sister. She is real and down-to-earth, and her comedic conversations and trendy jargon always keeps me laughing. I respect, understand and love her just as she is. Because she is constant, I know her and am comfortable with her. When my good friend began to walk with God, He began to shape her in a beautiful way. He gave her the afterglow. I call it the "afterglow" because after He gets on the inside and His light illuminates in, of, and about you, you have a spark that makes people inquisitive. It's the same when someone is falling in love: they begin to become a new creature. When love, rather true love abides, one begins to smile more, to say "yes" instead of "no," to open doors and say kinder things. With true love your confidence in life takes you to new levels, which completes and compliments you. Love is contagious, and people who are in love begin to love everybody. Things that usually are upsetting roll off your shoulder. In other words, where God says "to worry is a sin," in love you don't really worry. You are not bound by fear.

God asked us to love one another. How can we love an invisible God if we can't love our visible brothers and sisters? That is the gospel blueprint right there. Beyond and outside of His plan you will find fire, pain, hurt, disappointment, and abuse. Abuse comes in many forms and fashions. People will abuse you mentally, physically, emotionally, spiritually—they will use fear to do it. When you allow God to touch you with His love you will be unmovable and contagious bringing about light in dark places.

Charlotte had a great thirst for the truth, and I could see her zeal for the things of God. One of her greatest attributes is that she is a very real woman. She is light-hearted and powerful all in one; I appreciate her ability to be herself and serve God in harmony. Many people would question her "sanctification" based on her ability to be herself, to look and express herself the way she thinks is right in her service to God. Some people decide that you have to look a certain way and fit a certain mode in order to be saved, holy, and powerful. Most people would assume that Charlotte has no word in her, but let me tell you, when I am feeling depleted and worn, I turn to Charlotte, and she speaks the word of God, not her own agenda.

When people do me wrong, she reminds me who I am in God and how lovable our enemies ought to be. All the while she is as funny as ever, as encouraging and stylish, trendy and beautiful as ever. God called, and she answered the door, blinged out with four-inch heels, her oversized pocketbook, and her fabulous hair. And yet, she knows these things don't matter—her true treasure is her heart of gold.

Sometimes He wants to use you so that others recognize you and see His light accompanying you. I did not have to get to know the new Charlotte. I just have to see my good friend shine with a new "bling" (also known as Jesus!) that encircled her heart. Yes, He is some kind of bling! When Charlotte speaks of the Lord people are not put off; instead they are eager to learn of this peculiar change. We need to make sure as disciples of Christ we stay grounded and approachable in our faith—too much fanaticism could drive people from His light, rather than bring souls towards it.

Let's imagine that one day, I call Charlotte on the phone. "Praise the Lord, Sister Charlotte here…" She'd answer.

"Hi Charlotte," I would say."I wanted to tell you this hilarious story…" But before I could tell the story, Charlotte would interrupt.

"This is nothing but the devil that you would call me and disturb me during my prayer time." Imagine if she responded, angrily in that manner. Thank goodness Charlotte is not this way.

If that had happened, I would have been offended. It would have made me less inclined to speak with Charlotte in the future. But this kind of behavior, lacking discernment, compassion and love, is more common than you think. Believe me I have heard this time and time again. It can display a lack of spiritual sensitivity—what if the prayer summoned the call, or it was the appointed time to pray together? When you are yourself, God will receive you and you will certainly receive Him. Sincerity is powerful. Sincerity and true love is mighty!

Have you ever seen folks who complete every other sentence with "thank yah Jesus"? You say "Hello," and they respond all in one breath.

"I am fine thank the Lord. The kids are fine, thank yah Jesus, and I am moving right along in Jesus Praise God, I'm in school amen, working amen....praise the Lord and serving the Lord with my whole heart, Hallelujah Thank yah Jesus, in the name of Jesus, glory to God the head of my life."

When you are in a place of routine, it dictates the manner in which you pray and the manner in which you greet others, you are guilty of being "churchy." God is not routine, is not in a box, is not predictable, is not measurable, is not restricted and is not bound by religiosity. If you are striving towards His perfection, why should man dictate your personality, moreover your spiritual makeup? God made us unique because He likes us as we are, with our own features, fingerprints, and personalities.

Overly-churchy talk can leave your listener confused, sorting through all the push-button phrases, to try and discover the real person underneath all the Jesus garments. Make no mistakes, absolutely we should be proud of our Lord and Savior, absolutely we should give Him glory and honor, but there must be balance. God says in His word that we should not do anything in excess: "The man who fears God will avoid all extremes." [Ecclesiastes 7:18] God has not called us to appear as freaks or fanatics that overwhelm others with our own spiritual tornados. That is simply not God! When we cause people to run away from the gospel as a result of our extreme approach we become blood guilty. In God we can be beautiful, have a sense of humor, express our concern for things that are not settling in our spirit, laugh, let our hair down, forget to shave, eat to fullness, skip a meal, just be real. Just be plain ole me.

Being connected to God and deeply knowing the Lord requires first that you precede in pure love, and posses a sincere heart after His will. "Seek ye first the kingdom of God and His righteousness and all these things shall be added unto you." [Matthews 6:33] When you are at the point of walking closely with God, you have a sweetness that infuses your life completely. You look sweet and you are sweet, you have a sweet essence. In this mode of truth, you draw men by the inner light and the afterglow that comes from a true relationship with God the Father. Be a light both inside and outside the church. A conniving spirit and contemptuous heart accompanied with holy hands is suspect. It's like pouring sugar in hot sauce anticipating that its all good. Sadly, these people exist in high numbers. Don't let them lay hands on you—they need serious deliverance.

It is so beautiful when you can be yourself and be alright with who you are in God and what you were created for in God. One day I telephoned a relative. When he answered the phone he began to share an event with me and it went somewhat like this;

"I spoke with Sister So-and-So, amen and she said that she was going to try and push her way, amen to join us for prayer, amen and I told her, amen that if she felt up to it, amen we would be glad, amen to see her and her cousin, amen for service, amen.

God is moving, amen."

I looked at the phone receiver and mouthed "For real?" I had to let him know that he was overusing, misusing, and simply church-jacking the word "amen" a bit much for me.

"Hello. It's me, Ruby. Why this sudden change in personality?"

He said, "I know, I'm sorry. When I get into 'church mode' it just happens. I just get so excited about the Lord. I just got off the phone praying."

Why does there have to be a "church mode"? I thought. We should be living a Godly life in our skin comfortably, normally and with balance. I told him to

"Please decide which personality is yours so I can get used to one or the other," I told my relative. "I really liked the guy I met before; I did not sign up for the other one with the other mode." That was not very nice of me, I know, but he knows me, so it was well between us. When we fashion our personality around the ideal model for a saved person, we lose ourselves, and our footing in God. We can't alter His plans. We can't make up the rules as we go along either. God did already and He does not error, lie or cheat, He is perfect and His strength is made perfect in our weakness. You can rest assure when your walk reaches a degree of intimacy. This walk with God is not a joke. It is not about hide-and-go-seek either. You can't hide who you are behind words or false actions. Don't you know by now that God sees you and He hears you?

Before I go further, I want to pray, so that as I purpose to enlighten you, I don't injure anyone. The truth will set everybody free, so here goes...

Father in the precious name of Jesus, please guide me and order my words, my prayers and my delivery, father give me wisdom concerning your children. Lord-You-Your Word is perfect truth and Your Spirit which lives in the obedience of your children is our source and connection to you. Father I thank you for imparting your spirit and guiding us. Please keep us, protect us and enlighten us. Let your word be a light to my feet and a lamp to my path. Father in the name of Jesus, cover your true servants, messengers, presenters, teachers and preachers of your holiness. Father help us, your children to follow true doers of the word and not ravenous wolves that are set in high places to deceive us and destroy. Expose the enemy who is hiding behind your word and misleading your people. Free them from the clutches of the evil one. Give the pure in heart discerning spirits and the wisdom to free themselves from the bondage of spiritual whirlwinds that are sent to devastate the multitudes. Deliver the sick in spirit and bind the tactics of fear and control. Lord please guide me, as I go forth in this next area concerning churchy carbon copies, religious phonies and spiritual hypocrites. Lord I do not want to shed a negative light on the true people of God as they are your called children, thus they are exempt concerning what is to follow. Lord order my words so that clarity is precise and it falls on good and ready soil in the loving name of Jesus, Amen. Friend of mine, pray for clarity, discernment and guidance...

Heroes and stars are often esteemed as "special people." Many look up to them for the gifts that they posses, and aspire to be just like them. They get away with far more than the ordinary, as they are esteemed extraordinary and untouchable. Oddly when a "special person" breaks the rules or the law, he or she is privy to what we call double standards, exempting them from punishment. This reality today has taken a shift. I see the correction of more and more people in the spotlight than ever before. Leaders, teachers, politicians, ministers, celebrities, lawyers are being challenged in great numbers for various reasons. It is interesting how many people that partake in the gospel hide in the word to cover their mess.

Concerning the Children of God, good, bad, or indifferent, the stakes are higher. The word of God is nothing to take lightly. Today pastors are globalizing through media channels, promotion, and PR. This is truly a beautiful thing because it enables the reaching and teaching of the masses. The more you reach with the intent to set free, the more of you they scrutinize. Who sees? It is the believers and the non- believers, those of the light" as well as those of the dark. When you become a source of light, you become a target of particular interest and public scrutiny. There is a concrete difference in the word of God and entertainment however. Pastors are not sports figures, action figures, stars or entertainers. They are called to a humbling posture of strength with a greater accountability than entertainers. This is not a show, this is the real deal and one's soul is the vital factor. The word of God imparts that all fall short of the glory of God but it does not excuse us to habitual offense and the spirit of rebellion.

You have people who are in church three or more times a week, clapping and singing and tithing the whole nine, yet they are the meanest, most controlling and evil folks you will ever care to know. We see them in their Sunday's best going through all the seemingly spiritually connected motions, but the spirit of God is not with them. You have people leading and teaching and preaching and they are full of lust, addictions and unclean spirits. They have the spirit of pretentiousness, the spirit of denial, greed, confusion, delusion, error, vanity, sexual immorality, the spirit of hell and of the evil one. Careful! Know God and know His voice, don't follow foreigners in Christ. They are fakes, they are ravenous wolves, they are soul pimps, they are full of themselves they are called by Satan to destroy you, your house, your family, the church and your eternal gift. Protect yourself by walking closely with God; protect others by being real and true and showing them that they can come as they are to God. The peace, the joy, the love, the promise, the direction, the purpose all of it falls into place.

MY SHEEP KNOW MY VOICE AND A STRANGER THEY WILL NOT FOLLOW...

This is an important road to explore. After all the truth is what sets you free. What goes on behind the scenes would rock your world if you really knew about it. That is if you don't already know what time it is. Are you turning your cheek in error to your own detriment? Are you aware and in a mode of obliviousness? Are you caught up in a spiritual tornado in a midst absent of He who brings life and abundance because no one stands to agree? Are you walking with, talking with, supping with and resting with the evil ones? Are you on a scary-go-round bound by fear that immobilizes your God given good sense? Or are you walking in agreement, with the children of darkness? Which role is yours? Are you blind, unaware, in denial, afraid, uncertain, skeptic or guilty of partaking in the dark side?

Maybe you're presenting the "word" or sitting under the presenter of the "word," using it in vain for personal gain. This is "the danger zone." Get busy in prayer and pray much.

My mother use to say, "Ruby, wash your hands before you make a plate of food." Today I say if you are going to feed me, please wash your hands. I am saying repent before you handle the bread of my life. You find more deviant servants partaking in positions than you will find obedient servants. You find whoremongers and liars and thieves that are guilt-driven, running to the altar week after week. There are married folks who are active and willing adulterers, full of lust demons lifting up unholy hands, laying them on you, speaking in "push and play" audio tongues and all in the name of Jesus the Holy One. How dare they?!

The word itself says "out of the mouth of babes" comes the truth. That is because babies are not tainted, programmed, and corrupted. They can speak to God faster than many, and He hears them! I ask my eight-year-old son to pray for me all the time. We pray for one another; a family that prays together, stays together—we all know this to be true. He lays his little loving hands on me and begins to speak out of the essence of a pure heart. No -isms, no schisms, no ulterior motives, no conditions, no requirements, nothing complicated, nothing deep, no hoop, no automation, just pureness of heart and love for his Mom. I have faith and I have hope and I believe, that's enough, all things works together for the good because I love the Lord.

I am merely attempting to illustrate that if you want a personal relationship with someone and you want them to know you for whom you are, you have to be yourself and walk with them until you feel the bond. Walking intimately with God is all about sincerity; it's all about opening up to God the Father. The truth is, power comes from praying and seeking God in all things. That means you must, you have no choice, you must be a vessel of love to get to the power and to keep the power. No exemptions, nothing qualifies you to be exempt from loving everyone, like them or leave them, in the name of Jesus, you have to genuinely love them. If you want a true relationship with God then the best thing to do is to start out by simply being yourself. You will be just fine.

I dedicate this chapter to a young girl appropriately named Jewel Burnette. Jewel has been filled with the Holy Spirit and is authentically in love with her creator. May you, little one remain precious, seen and read as a vessel of true faith. I pray that someone watching is inspired by the beauty of the Christ in you.

CHAPTER 17

Faith

J esus taught, "I tell you the truth, if you have faith as small as a mustard seed, you can say to this mountain, 'Move from here to there' and it will move. Nothing will be impossible for you." [Matthew 17:20] A mustard seed is proportionately minute. In fact, if you beheld a mustard seed and dropped it in a field, you would experience a great challenge in locating the seed. When God said that such small faith could move mountains, one can only imagine what blazing faith could do. He knew in advance that it would be difficult for most to believe that which they could not see.

In John Chapter 20 the writer explores seeing and believing. Thomas was called the Twin, one of the twelve disciples of Christ, referred to also as doubting Thomas. In scripture we learn of how the other disciples share that they had seen the Lord. However, Thomas said he would not believe that Christ rose again until he saw the nail prints in his hand. When Christ appeared amongst the disciples, he said to Thomas, "Place your hand in my side so that you now believe. You have seen and now you believe, but blessed are they who have not seen anything and yet believe." [John 20:24,5]

If we had to rely on a visual to get us to the Promise Land, we would surely fail. You will find a commonality amongst people who achieve goals and live dreams. The common thread amongst those living their purpose is the drive, the fire but most importantly, the faith. People tend to believe in the promise so much that they go after it never considering failure or doubting success. Those are the ones that have walked by Faith and not by sight! When God implied that the race is not given to the swift, we can attest that many will take off running concerning something they want but they burn out and lose the spark to finish with the same momentum that got them started. God said the race is given to the ones that endure until the end. Endurance will allow you to go forward in spite of obstacles and hindrances. Your focus is fixated on the promises of God therefore enduring is not the best thing to do, but the only thing to do. Faith will keep your head straight and keep you from sinking along the way. In faith there is no limit, all can be achieved, so long as it is the will of God.

Faith is the birthing place of power and by His spirit we are empowered to do ALL things. The word "all" is invariably used time and time again in the Holy Scriptures. All is expressed as the whole of one's possessions, resources and energy. Who enables us to gain possessions? And with whom do our resources abide? God indeed energize us; give us strength, hope, and the power to navigate physically, mentally and spiritually. He is the alpha and the omega. He is all power and all knowing. He is Love. The Lord is everything beautiful, everything pure.

You, much like a bed of roses, have become what you are as the result of many factors. You have been shaped and fertilized by learned behavior, biological predisposition, environment, culture, genetics, and belief-systems and etc. What seeds have been planted, fertilized, watered and cropped within you? Plant those Faith seeds and man your post, it is going to be all right, I promise. I promise by Faith! I believe when we get our thinking in order, things will balance according to our new and clean state of mind. Again and again, where the mind goes the body follows.

Learn to meditate on God and His Word. By meditating on God's Word you will find joy, peace, prosperity, long life and a real relationship with God. "Does a fountain at the same place send forth sweet water and bitter? Can the fig tree, my brethren, bare olive berries either a vine, of figs? So can no fountain both yield salt water and fresh." [James 3:11,12]

Your words are important and should be spoken in wisdom: "Wise men lay up knowledge: but the mouth of the foolish is near destruction." [Proverbs 10:14] It is not what goes into a mouth that defiles man, but what comes out of his mouth. Words represent the heart of man, as he thinks, so he is. "The mouth of a righteous man is a well of life: but violence covereth the mouth of the wicked." [Proverbs 10:11] Use wisdom! For every idle word spoken must be accounted for. Take a true account of where you stand today and begin to apply the principles of God to your life. So by the power of faith and the baring of love you may be made whole and be victorious over all things.

You ever hear the saying *less is more?* Or, *a wise man is of few words, but a fool is of many?* Why not try getting more wisdom around faith so that when you speak in faith, you speak life by applying the Word you have digested? Try this exercise for me: don't open your mouth until you learn to practice these thoughts in your mind. Do this for yourself and for others and the seeds will be planted. Once they are planted, speak life to your heart's content. There is both life—and death—in the power of the tongue.

I would like to reflect upon the faithful prayer of Jabez for a moment. This prayer can be found in I Chronicles, Chapter 4. In verse 10, Jabez prayed specifically by calling on the God of Israel, saying, "Oh that Thou wouldest bless me indeed, and enlarge my coast, and that Thine hand might be with me, and that Thou wouldest keep me from evil, that it may not grieve me!" God granted him that which he requested. One thing I notice about this prayer is that it is concise, but concentrated. The prayer was passionate and held great anticipation. Jabez fully expected his prayer to be answered, because of his faith in the Father. There are four requests in his prayer. He asks God to bless him, he asks God to enlarge his territory or increase his responsibility, he asks God to be with him, and finally he asks God to keep him from harm. God wants us to turn to Him in all that we do. In the tenderness of our need He will answer and bless us. Jabez clearly understands that there is only one God with whom he has anchored his hope in. Learn how to cry out in great expectation to God the Father. When you pray often, you make rich, your relationship with God. When you pray believing, you build your faith. When you pray trusting, you can walk away from the problem and walk with the problem solver. "For they cried to God in the battle and he was entreated of them because they put their trust in Him." 1 Chronicles 5:20] God answered their prayers because they trusted in Him.

Below we can pray this way:

I shall not die but live, my vision and God's perfect will for my life shall not die but live! My dreams shall live, my joy shall live, my health shall stand rich and full of vitality, my circumstances are full of glory and of life, my love ones shall live in health, joy and prosperity of peace and finances, my finances shall weather the storms and prosper back unto me, by active faith and by God's Might and His Glory and His promises to me, by the substance and evidence I see and anticipate…all while giving him glory in totality with my every breath and committed heart-- I claim that my purpose shall not be cursed, my transformation shall not be derailed but alive. And through the life words that go out from my mouth, fashioned with purpose landing upon a pre-fertilized and fruitful destination like Jabez prayed for a break through to a blessed and extraordinary life, "Oh that you would bless me indeed and enlarge my territory." I claim that ever-increasing territory, I pray that your favor rain on me and your grace and mercy light and guard the ground upon which I must tread, Lord I need a ram in the bush…Father I humble myself and pray, I speak your name asking for forgiveness as I repent day after day. Grant me the strength to rise up the spirit in this man and turn from the ways of failing flesh. Father, hear from heaven and heal thy land. Greater are you in me than I could ever possibly be in the world. I can't go without your covering. Lord be with me and with you I can do all things…be beyond a conqueror. I am a child of the most High God and He said….just knock child and so I am now knocking [and the door just opened], He said seek son, seek daughter and Daddy my eyes are gazed upon you, they are on the sparrow and I am here to claim my territory and be victorious in you. Fear! I dismiss you now. Bye bye bye bye, I don't work for you anymore, I don't serve you either, nor am I your slave, I divorce you, it's over now. The sky has no limit… and I have wings that work just fine. You have your proper place and I commit you back to the dry place from whence you've come! You are not the boss of me and you don't dictate my destiny! I can't keep you in my garden anymore…..Faith without works is dead and that is why I am activating it now, cause its alive, its alive its alive and it is working for me, in me, on me and all around me. Now be gone in the matchless name of Jesus!

Your praise and worship will annihilate every insurrection of fear that attempts to dwell in your existence. Fear will yield, will bow, and will scatter in the presence of God's Glory. The more you exalt him the more you will see evidence of shackles breaking around you. You will be free indeed.

STOP READING!

Begin to exalt and praise and lift up His Holy name. Thank him for giving you victory over the fear that kept you bound from your purpose. Return to this inspiration when you are ready, and when He releases you to it.

Faith

Record here, what you have learned and how you will apply it to your life:

_____

_____

_____

_____

_____

_____

_____

_____

_____

_____

_____

_____

_____

_____

_____

_____

_____

_____

FEAR IS NOT MY BOSS

Record here, your good and perfect prayer concerning faith over fear. With it, you will be able to help someone who is at the bed of fear.

_____

_____

_____

_____

_____

_____

_____

_____

_____

_____

_____

_____

_____

_____

_____

_____

_____

In faith speak this…

> *Fear **is not my boss**. Fear **will not control my life**. Fear **has to bow to faith**. Fear **is the little guy and faith is the big guy. I choose faith. I choose faith. I choose faith.** Fear **has no place in my life.** Fear **will not predicate my future.** Fear **is the voice of the past. I curse** fear **at the root and send it to dry places. I bind** fear **in heaven and on earth I loose that I am more than a conquerer delivered from the spirit of fear and in authority I take back my life, my freedom and my joy from the clutches of fear in the matchless name of Jesus. Amen…Glory to God…Hallelieujah.**

Welcome back prayer warrior! Welcome back exalter! Return with vigor and the authority to move mountainous fear out of your path. You see obedience is key! Claim that fear is no more, and fear shall be no more. Exhale, smile for me, then read onward!

Fear is responsible for everything negative—on the receiving end and the producing end. Being mean, for example, is in the spirit of meanness. It can influence our entire body-mind-spirit being in a negative way. Let us ponder upon a mere frown. When we frown over a period of time, it has an adverse effect on our posture, expression, and our image. It is known that frowning causes permanent, unwanted lines in the face that can only be medically reversed. Frowning further sends a signal to the brain that correlates with the emotion of discontent or dissatisfaction, even anger. Once our mental and physical state partner, our spirit becomes toxic, and we produce sour fruits of the spirit. When we allow this emotion to rule our time and space, we somehow learn to live in a toxic environment that internally eats away at our ability to be clear and be happy in general.

If you trace back and discover what the underlying cause of anger, hostility, or negative energy, you may find that fear is ultimately responsible for most, if not all, of these behaviors. People tend to fear that if they appear too kind, too soft, or too giving, they will be taken advantage of or used. The key to joyful living is to be good, kind, and loving, through sound judgment, which comes by seeking and praying for wisdom. When you are bitter and mean, you do it on purpose. Kindness is much easier, as one must go out of the way to be unkind. What baby is born unkind? That is something we learn to do in and of ourselves. We can depend on the gift of love to carry us through and cover us too! With love, faith is empowered.

Fear is in the eye of the beholder! What paralyzes you may empower someone else. Children typically fear the dark because they can not see. But this fear comes about through what we learn. The fetus is formed in the dark and is quite content there. An infant is peaceful in the dark and in the light, he has not learned to fear. Once learned, the dark is symbolic of the unknown, compared most commonly to death. However, in the dark life began and all was formed. Many people fear death and see it as a dark cold place that is final. Death is perpetually deemed "the unknown" hence fear super imposes the life transition beyond death. When we nurture our walk and relationship with our creator, we gain insight, wisdom and power over fear, particularly the unknown. We spiritually mature and place our hope beyond hope and confidence in the substance of things hoped for and the evidence of things unseen. We learn to walk in the spirit or by Faith, not by sight. We exercise our trust, temperance, and Faith day after day helping us to rise above fear.

CHAPTER 18

Scenarios

"I WILL NOT ABANDON YOU OR LEAVE YOU AS
ORPHANS IN THE STORM—I WILL COME TO YOU."
[John 14:18]

"Consider it *pure joy, my brothers, whenever you face
trials of many kinds, because you know that the testing of
your faith develops perseverance.*" [James 1:2-3]

We are in the world but not of the world. This gives us
a renewed perspective towards where we are heading
rather, than that which we are facing. The storms in
life will present themselves to you, but you will not face them alone.
As you weather the storms in life you can be certain that God will
never leave you or forsake you. In the midst of your storm, you must
gaze your heart upon the promises of God in faith and complete
confidence that He is going to carry you through it. Ask Him in the

storm to reveal what you must get out of the storm. Get the value out of the valley by turning to God who is an ever-present help in times of trouble.

Has anyone attempted to or been successful at controlling you through fear? This kind of control can be found at home, in school, in the work place, on the streets, in the prisons, hospitals, even the church. People that allow flesh to control their destiny usually have blurry spiritual vision and so they use control to gain power. They control others by inflicting fear; they are able to control and shape your thinking through adulterating your beliefs. Remember that the gift of Life is Free, because it was paid for in advance for you and for me. You should never be bound to man, by any means. However, where there is commitment or an agreement on one accord, working toward a vision or the better good, this is different.

Here are some common fear scenarios, and how to combat them:

I am under stress at work and I am afraid I am going to loose my job?

Instead of fueling fear, use the fear as fuel to step up your game, no matter the circumstances. Apply that same energy in new training, new ideas, and new methods. When you perform in the spirit of excellence, it never goes unnoticed. Even if you think nobody is watching, I assure you He is. So remember to perform at peak, have faith, pray much and witness the growth in your territory....you will be either compensated, rewarded and/or blessed. Fear NOT!

I can't leave my job, I don't have a degree or the credentials to make it.

Just stop. You are who you confess you are. Are you more are you more than a conqueror or not? Pray to God for direction and ask him to provide a ram or two in the bush for you, so that you may go forward by his favor. God is no respecter of persons so when the wind blows favor on others, you get some of it too. Keep good company so that the wind is blowing the right stuff at the right time in the right way. Faith without works is dead. Try coupling prayer with a marketing plan for you to make your grand exit and great entrance into your new destiny.

I have a health battle and it does not look good and I am afraid that .....

Shhhhhhh...Don't even say it! Don't speak seeds of defeat. Rewrite your script, make revisions and revamp your role in this case. You are free indeed and by His stripes made whole and healed. Remember this: *where the mind goes, the body follows! As a man thinketh, so is he!* Condition your thinking to ponder upon everything beautiful.

My marriage is failing and I have tried everything....

When you get done trying, hustling, experimenting, get out of the way and let God do His thing. All you have to do is stop trying to change yourself through someone else. The things you want so desperately to fix in your mate are usually your own faults, your own errors and your own mess. Once married, two become one...so work on yourself and your mate will respond. Fear gets in the fiber and fragments of our relationship, causing discomfort and irritation. Together be sweet, loving and kind, be respectful to self and others. Stormy O'Martin has a powerful read: *The Power of a Praying Wife* and *The Power of a Praying Husband.* Go get those books—they bare great fruit!

There are enumerable attacks you may have experienced or witnessed in your life, too many to name. The enemy uses anything and anyone he can to strategically approach your intended demise. I don't want you to underestimate the snares of the fowler for one minute. Be clear: he is not your friend, though often, he pretends to be just that. He has a way with using others knowing and unknowingly, that they are being used of him. This is why wisdom and sensitivity are areas in which we must pray for growth. I would not want to take place in the enemies plot to bring severe disaster to anyone, love them or leave them. We should pray for our enemy and love them. The storms in your life are not exempt, they two are on a clock and must obey God. Once you begin to accept the authority that you are given as children of the most high God, you will understand that you can speak in faith, to the events in your life and change things, according to the word of God.

CHAPTER 19

Power from Heaven

BUT WE HAVE THIS TREASURE IN EARTHEN VESSELS, THAT THE EXCELLENCY OF THE POWER MAY BE OF GOD AND NOT OF US

In the beginning was the Word, and the Word was with God, and the Word was God. "Yet for us there is only one God, the Father, from whom everything came into being and for whom we live. And there is only one Lord, Jesus the Messiah, through whom everything came into being and through whom we live." [1 Corinthians 8:6] The same was in the beginning with God. All things were made by Him; and without Him was not any thing made that was made. In Him was life; and the life was the light of men. The "Word" is the expression of God's heart, mind and will. In the "Word" likewise in Him are both truth and life. Through the light of the life is the power to defeat the forces and plagues of darkness: "Seek ye first the kingdom of God, and his righteousness; and all these things shall be added unto you." [Matthew 6:33]

Our mission is to be unified with The Holy One. Though we are born again, it is important that we seek the full knowledge of God, the Holy One. Of primary importance, we must pray for understanding concerning the knowledge we receive as wisdom follows. In Proverbs 1:7 we are taught about the fear of the Lord: "The fear of the Lord is the beginning of knowledge, but fools despise wisdom and instruction." In Proverbs 9:10 it furthers by sharing, "The fear of the Lord is the beginning of wisdom, and the knowledge of the Holy One is understanding."

As we have been reminded, without Faith it is impossible to please God. We are also aware that Faith without works is dead. That means that God holds us accountable to active faith. God requires us to take action concerning our relationship with Him by believing in him. We can't just expect Him to come looking for us. We are the ones that lost our way and He is our way. We are cordially invited to His courts that He may dwell in us. He is not lost; He is patiently waiting for us to reciprocate the love that He gives so freely. He requires us to do something. In His word we are reminded simply to ask, seek, knock. For everyone who asks receives, who seeks finds and whom ever knocks will find an open door.

"To ask that you may be filled with the knowledge of His will in all wisdom and spiritual understanding; that you may have a walk worthy of the Lord, fully pleasing Him, being fruitful in every good work and increasing in the knowledge of God." [Colossians 1:9] Wisdom gives life to those who pursue the excellence of knowledge. *Know this, God is God alone!*

We call Him...

Adonai-Jehovah—The Lord our Sovereign

El-Elyon—The Lord Most High

El-Olam—The Everlasting God

El-Shaddai—The God Who is Sufficient for the Needs of His People

Elohim—The Eternal Creator

Jehovah-Jireh—The Lord our Provider

Jehovah-Nissi—The Lord our Banner

Jehovah-Ropheka—The Lord our Healer

Jehovah-Shalom—The Lord our Peace

Jehovah-Tsidkenu—The Lord our Righteousness

Jehovah-Mekaddishkem—The Lord our Sanctifier

Jehovah-Sabaoth—The Lord of Hosts

Jehovah-Shammah—The Lord is Present

Jehovah-Rohi—The Lord our Shepherd

Jehovah-Hoseenu—The Lord our Maker

Jehovah-Eloheenu—The Lord our God.

God is infinite, He is eternal, He had no beginning and for Him there is no end. He is immutable, constant. He is perfect, just, incorruptible. God is worthy to be praised. Praising Him and worshipping Him proves powerful in all instances. Praise God when times are good and praise him when times are rough. By praising Him through your difficult events you will transpose the atmosphere by ushering in His glory. There is absolute power in praise:

> *Bless the Lord, O my soul, O Lord my God, thou art very great; thou art clothes with honour and majesty; Who coverest thyself with light as with garment; Who stretchest out the heavens like a curtain; Who layeth the beams of his chambers in the waters; who maketh the clouds His chariot; who walketh upon the wings of the wind; Who maketh his angels spirits his ministers a flaming fire; Who laid the foundations of the earth, that it should not be removed for ever. Thou coveredst it with the deep as with a garment; the waters stood above the mountains. At thy rebuke they fled; at the voice of they thunder they hasted away. He watereth the hills from his chambers: the earth is satisfied with the fruit of thy works. The glory of the Lord shall endure for ever: the Lord shall rejoice in his works. I will sing unto the Lord as long as I live: I will sing praise to my God while I have my being. My meditation of him shall be sweet: I will be glad in the Lord. [Psalms 104:1-34]*

So many people seek the power of God (Selah) but it is better to seek God; the power will follow. Do you believe that God will reward those that diligently seek Him? I do, I believe that if I seek God wholeheartedly, He will equip me, anoint me and appoint me to do great things. Not great things for my own satisfaction, but great things for His glory. The use of your gift in humility, service and glorification of the gospel will bring about development in that area, breathing life on your call to ministry where your gift will make room for you. God is imparting your call to duty.

Next from Matthew 25:14-30 is an example concerning gifts. Gifts are broad in range and can be in the area of leadership, instruction, prayer warrior, healer, interpreter, psalmist, musician, fisher of men, story telling, writing, inspiring, encouraging, forgiveness, love, kindness, help, you name it. Whatever gifts God has given you and anointed you for, is by His hand, of His might and for His glory. With that being said we are required to use those gifts fully in service to one another and to His Glory and Honor.

Parable Found in Matthew 25:

> A man going on a journey called his servants and entrusted his property to them. To one he gave five talents of money, to another two talents, and to another one talent, each according to his ability. Then he went on his journey. The man who had received the five talents went at once and put his money to work and gained five more. So also, the one with the two talents gained two more. But the man who had received the one talent went off, dug a hole in the ground and hid his master's money.

> After a long time the master of those servants returned and settled accounts with them. The man who had received the five talents brought the other five. "Master," he said, "you entrusted me with five talents. See,

I have gained five more."

His master replied, "Well done, good and faithful servant! You have been faithful with a few things; I will put you in charge of many things. Come and share your master's happiness!"

The man with the two talents also came. "Master," he said, "you entrusted me with two talents; see, I have gained two more."

His master replied, "Well done, good and faithful servant! You have been faithful with a few things; I will put you in charge of many things. Come and share your master's happiness!"

Then the man who had received the one talent came. "Master," he said, "I knew that you are a hard man, harvesting where you have not sown and gathering where you have not scattered seed. So I was afraid and went out and hid your talent in the ground. See, here is what belongs to you."

His master replied, "You wicked, lazy servant! So you knew that I harvest where I have not sown and gather where I have not scattered seed? Well then, you should have put my money on deposit with the bankers, so that when I returned I would have received it back with interest. Take the talent from him and give it to the one who has the ten talents. For everyone who has will be given more, and he will have an abundance. Whoever does not have, even what he has will be taken from him. And throw that worthless servant outside, into the darkness, where there will be weeping and gnashing of teeth."

Perhaps you have not yet discovered what your spiritual gift is but so long as you are connected to the gift giver, in time it will be revealed. All the while saturate yourself in His presence as He permeates the atmosphere with His Spirit. How? Pray, Ask, Seek, knock, Share, Exchange, Worship and do all that you can to experience the presence of God so that you may be able to hear what He is saying. When the gift you operate in has the full manifestation of the Spirit of God through holy living, it is deemed powerful. You receive this power from heaven when you surrender to God in full faith, total obedience, humility and love. You walk in the authority of power through pureness of heart. When you have the power of God on your side, you can walk in the authority expecting full victory.

Here's the flip side to this: when you make a promise to God, giving your life over to Him, seeking the full knowledge, you become an annoyance to the enemy of your soul. If you are serious about your commitment, the enemy will try everything under the sun to derail you. During such attacks, you will need to remain close to God, who will war for you. It can be very difficult, during this wilderness experience, but if you stay focused, you will make it through. "For God gives power to the faint and to them that have might He increases strength." [Isaiah 40:29] God will remain with you.

Jesus came out of the wilderness filled with the Holy Spirit and so can you. He proclaimed that you would do greater works. He bestowed the same power upon His people. He worked miracles and wonders by the might of compassion and faith as He healed the sick, made the blind to see, the mute to hear, the dead to rise, the lame to walk, He delivered and He set free. He redeemed us, died, rose again, atoned for our sins and forgave us in our ignorance and error. His capacity to love is pure holiness and it is endless. He said He would be with us even until the end. It is by His Spirit and in His likeness that we will operate as agents for Christ.

True power is not absent of great sacrifice. To perform in this capacity you must be strong, full of faith, pure at heart, touched by God, sent by God, and sure of your election. You must be disciplined and steadfast enough to trust God through the season of lack, storms, and whatever may come. If you want the power to perform great works such as healing, delivering, setting free, you should know that the requirements are great. More specifically, the requirements may require that you be stripped, broken, whipped, kicked, falsely accused, attacked, left behind. There is a cost in discipleship and one should consider his or her sufficiency. Are you about God's business with all of you heart, mind and soul?

As Jesus was tried in the wilderness, He did not eat or drink for forty days and forty nights. He depended solely on the Word of His Father for manna. Just as His wilderness season was ending, the enemy came to tempt Him suggesting; "if you are a son of God command that these stones become bread." [Matthew 4:3] Then in wisdom and trust Christ responded "man should not live by bread alone but by every word that proceeds from the mouth of God." [Matthew 4: 4] In other words, when we are seeking God for direction and wisdom, we must understand that He will speak, He will answer, He will touch, He will. However, we must be patient and diligent, operating in wisdom as we are tried and tested in our wilderness season, even up to the point of power. Before you even discover what God has for you, the devil is in his workshop plotting to steal it from you. He is working to kill your purpose before it can be birthed.

Think about this: when Jesus was in the wilderness, he was not asking God questions like, *why am I here?* Or *how can I get out of this situation?* He was not depressed about his situation. But if you note the posture of Christ, you will see that He trusted God fully. He depended on God for everything; he used His time in wisdom by fasting, praying and resisting the enemy's temptations.

Not everyone will go through life completely trusting God all of the time. Some will doubt, fall to temptation, even become angry with the situation or even angry with God while in the wilderness. It is your attitude that makes the difference in what comes of your wilderness season. A correct attitude will birth the correct aptitude. I know that it is hard to be in peace, especially when you focus on the pain. In spite of it, I dare you to proceed in faith through your storm, leaning and trusting in God the Almighty One.

CHAPTER 20

For You III

I HAVE PROVIDED WORDS TO MEDITATE ON
AND A JOURNAL TO RECORD YOUR PERSONAL
EXPERIENCES.

EXERCISE

Meditate on the fragrance of Jesus. Deeply inhale the essence of His sweetness and His embrace. Concentrate on the love of Jesus and envision yourself resting in His arms. Focus on and remain faithful in the power in His name and the strength of His eternal glory. Surrender and escape in the peace and stillness of an unfailing God. Release all of your burdens with each fleeting breath and celebrate the many blessings that He has bestowed upon you as you breathe within. Picture a warm moderate breeze cleansing you with freedom and celebrate in that intimate moment with the Lord. For He has established you.

Record what your burdens and struggles may be or have been and then cross them out. Replace them with affirmations of victory over the hurdles you've provided. Highlight the affirmations that you've released as words that will prosper back unto you and yours. Here too, use a florescent marker and give this over to God who is ultimately in control of your life. We all have hurdles and hills to climb but we must not allow them to move us.

List your burdens, struggles, and storms,
then cross them out here:

_____

_____

_____

_____

_____

_____

_____

_____

_____

_____

_____

_____

_____

_____

_____

_____

List your affirming words of power here:

_____

_____

_____

_____

_____

_____

_____

_____

_____

_____

_____

_____

PART IV

Love

CHAPTER 21

Higher Obedience in Love

In the New Testament, we are called higher to obedience, '"Love the Lord your God with all your heart and with all your soul and with all your mind." [Matthew 22:36-40] This is the first and greatest commandment. We are called to walk in the beauty and grace of love concerning all things. Our total being is called to adhere to the power of love? What is this thing called love? How do we measure it?

The dictionary offers the following definitions for love:

- strong affection for another arising out of kinship or personal ties

- attraction based on sexual desire; affection and tenderness felt by lovers

- affection based on admiration, benevolence, or

common interests

- warm attachment, enthusiasm, or devotion

- unselfish loyal and benevolent concern for the good of another

- a person's adoration of God

- an amorous episode or a sexual embrace

There are so many different expressions of love. There is love as an emotion and there is love in its perfect form. Love as an emotion is not dependable because emotions are not stable. They change from day to day, even moment to moment. They are magnified or compromised pending our feelings and sentiment. Notice that, it is commonly said that women are more emotional (sentimental) than men. With this being probable, it would be safe to say that women love harder and stronger, but inconsistently. It would be difficult to trust love that is emotionally based. Could a marriage last on the premise of unstable emotions, or could a child depend completely on a parent that had only the emotional form of love to give? God's love, however, is perfect. It does not fluctuate, it remains unchanging, unwavering and unmovable. God's Love is *unconditional!*

Love is offered in the Greek language in three expressions. *Eros* refers to the love between a man and a woman: a passionate, physical love. The second form of love is *Phileo,* the expression of friendship, parental or family love. Finally, there is *Agape* love, which is love in the highest form. Agape love is love in perfection, stable and unmovable. This is the form of love that God is and God gives. This gift of love is the love that God decrees that we give to one another. The

Apostle Paul imparted that this love was, is and will forever remain, the greatest of all gifts, because it will never die. In this gift of perfect love, Agape love, there are no blemishes or areas of weakness. Love is the fruit of the spirit. We too are to bare such fruit—perfect love. In doing so, even the most fearful person will discover the bridge to escape the wilderness of fear. There is a bridge, I know. Love is that bridge, the way out of bondage. Love is the ultimate power. It is above and beyond fear. It is stronger than Fear! In the spirit of love you are more than a conqueror because love conquers fear.

If you can understand that you can conquer your fears and doubts through Christ your strength, then you have a winner's spirit. God offers a way of escape and an answer to all of our concerns. The Word of God addresses every aspect of our lives. Fear is not of God, rather power and love and a stable mind. Apostle Paul wrote...

> *If I speak in the tongues of men and of angels, but have not love, I am only a resounding gong or a clanging cymbal. If I have the gift of prophecy and can fathom all mysteries and all knowledge, and if I have a faith that can move mountains, but have not love, I am nothing. If I give all I possess to the poor and surrender my body to the flames, but have not love, I gain nothing. Love is patient, love is kind. It does not envy, it does not boast, it is not proud. It is not rude, it is not self-seeking, it is not easily angered, it keeps no record of wrongs. Love does not delight in evil but rejoices with the truth. It always protects, always trusts, always hopes, always, perseveres. Love never fails. But where there are prophecies, they will cease; where there are tongues, they will be stilled; where there is knowledge, it will pass away. For we know*

in part and we prophesy in part, but when perfection comes, the imperfect disappears. When I was a child, I talked like a child, I thought like a child, I reasoned like a child. When I became a man, I put childish ways behind me. Now we see but a poor reflection as in a mirror; then we shall see face to face. Now I know in part; then I shall know fully, even as I am fully known. And now these three remain: faith, hope and love. But the greatest of these is love. [1 Corinthians 1-13]

God loves us so much that He showers us with love and gives us each gifts and calling. God purposed, fashioned, gifted and called you before He formed the foundations of this earth. There is a scripture that reads "Many are called, but few are chosen." [Matthews 22:14] The few that are not chosen, opted out. You are given a choice in your free will. It is God's intent that we would all prosper, in health and not perish. Contrarily, we opt to live in sin and ignore the call, forfeiting eternal life by ignoring the prevailing gift of love.

To one there is given through the Spirit the message of wisdom, to another the message of knowledge by means of the same Spirit, to another faith by the same Spirit, to another gifts of healing by that one Spirit, to another miraculous powers, to another prophecy, to another distinguishing between spirits, to another speaking in different kinds of tongues, and to still another the interpretation of tongues. All these are the work of one and the same Spirit, and he gives them to each one, just as he determines. [Corinthians 12:8] What God gives, He does not take back, the gifts and the calling are irrevocable. God's Word reads in this way, for gifts and callings are without repentance. [Romans 11:29]. What does this mean? This means that people who operate in the gift may be in or out of God's good and perfect will for their life. "Through love and faithfulness sin is atoned for; through the fear of the Lord a man avoids evil." [Proverbs 16:6] Look for love, hope and faith, see the gift, but look for the anointing. Look for the spirit of God. If you have been mightily gifted and you have discovered your purpose, don't forfeit your blessings, by perverting your gifts... this is a poor example of gratitude.

In life, we may give someone something and when they disappoint us, we consider taking it back. Listen up, when you want something back, you never really gave; rather, you gave conditionally. Giving should be done in the spirit of humility. It is a private matter. When you give someone something you should not run and tell it on the mountain. If you tell, your gift is not recorded in the book of good deeds. God loves a cheerful giver and it is better to give than to receive. Love is the key; love is a prerequisite to all things. When you give out of love and someone intentionally hurts or abuses you, trust me, they need those drops and remnants of the love you released more than you do "Touch not my anointed and do my prophet no wrong," [Psalm 105:15] is that not the Word? "Anointed" means Christ. That means in order to be anointed you must have the spirit of Christ indwelling. If you have Christ on the inside, you have His anointing. If you have Christ and His anointing, you must have love, there is no either or in this. That gift of love that you gave may minister to them at some later point and time.

Whatever you have to do to get it on the inside, which is where it counts, do it. Love on the surface is not love, it's of another persuasion and this is dangerous. When you deal with surface love, it is privy to varying spirits and curses. In the midst of surface love, you will find envy, jealousy, and hate that wants to turn you upside down and inside out. The enemy, the father of everything destructive, wants to scrape you with a fine tooth comb, leaving no good crop to harvest. He wants to occupy you with the kind of love that is subject to emotions, where anything can happen and will eventually tear you into pieces, but love! Love conquers all, including fear. Seek agape love, allowing it to permeate your existence. The enemy will fool you with forms of love that are a set up and a set back. Live, teach and give love in an unconditional way.

There is a song I love that is relevant...*There is something about love; that scares me, there's something about caring too much. Well maybe I'm afraid I'm not giving enough, or perhaps I am taking much too much, but teach me I want to learn, how to love but nobody can take this away no, no, no, its something about Love!* I just love this song. See it's good to be honest and say, "Okay, I see in my carnal mind." Just don't be bound by the natural man. The writer offers "there's something about love that scares me...something about caring too much." Imagine how God feels, giving us all this love and we betray Him, walk away form Him, we disappoint Him and hurt Him.

We come for a season and then leave after He heals us. No one said you would not feel this time and again. Look at the innocence when the writer questions "maybe I'm afraid I'm not giving enough." The writer wants to be sure that he is going about loving in the manner and posture of God. But in the writer's expression of love we can see that in spite of fear, go on, for great is your reward. When you walk in love, and pray for the Lord to grant you a teachable spirit and a pliable heart whereby no one can take it away.

I yield to the power of love, hope and faith in Christ.

222

Through Christ and His wonder working power I speak agape love over every angle of the enemies plan to make us turn away from love. I curse that spirit of fear at the root, at the route, at the core and along its pathways. I bind it here on earth as it is bound in heaven and I loose the cure here on earth as it is loosed in heaven, giving no ground for the enemy to destroy this body through the two way spirit of fear. In the matchless name of Jesus, I call on the power of love that cometh from God Himself. I in faith curse fear at the root and send it to dry places. I rebuke the sin of my flesh and command that it come under the submission of God's Word and Will for my life. God speak to the winds that I may encounter favor from the north the south the east and the west. Blow wind blow—springing forth the unchanging love of God that it would encamp around me and teach me continually how to love. Amen.

While writing this section on love, I was put in a situation where several people that were close to me, hurt me. I had briefly decided to write off these folks and keep it moving. How many of us know and hear the voice of God? He will tug on your spirit man and show you just who and where you are in a situation that He wants to get the glory out of. You see if God gets the glory, you can be certain that everything and everybody will be alright. In doing so, you will find that you can't just cut folks off without being a hypocrite to love. When you begin to really get this and understand that true love will never die, you will find that the gift and power of love is the only way to make it, period.

During this area of work, my husband hurt me so, I felt he disrespected me and I was hurt. He pierced so deeply that at first, I honestly did not know I was cut. God was working on me and in me, so His grace kept me in a beautiful way. I was able to handle this in love, so I thought. However when we got home, we were cordial. I thought to myself, *I am tired of being disappointed and I really considered throwing in the towel.* But when I returned to the work here on the ministry concerning love, I was not able to go on. The Lord dropped a pearl on my spirit: someone sent a text message to me that said simply: Love covers all things. When I got this I instantly realized that I was out of God's will and He needed me to see myself. Sunday then came, and in service Bishop Ferrell preached on the prevailing gift of forgiveness so specifically, I thought, *Okay Okay Okay Lord, I surrender. I am getting out of flesh and in the spirit where you can first heal me, then strengthen me, finally use me and most importantly get the glory.* I told my husband that I love him and I care. He told me that he loved me and to be encouraged. Realize that a test will surely come. A storm will certainly come, but God loves you and will make sure you are fit for whatever comes. He wants you to grow up and get this love so fitted down on the inside that after the storm, love still stands. It has to stand the test of time.

Once you turn up the volume concerning love, it feels so good, renewed and free. It is easy to love who you love—that doesn't require much work at all. True deliverance takes place when you remove the parameters of earthly love and you supernaturally, supersede earthly levels by tapping into the heavenly love that has been ordained by God. We call this "perfect love". Perfect love will allow you to love those that trespass against you. Yes, if we want to be forgiven, we must first learn to forgive, even if we are right and the person is wrong. Pray like this…

Our father [mine and yours] which art in heaven, [He is on the throne] hollowed by thy name [He is Holy] thy kingdom come [God will make everything beautiful in His time] thy will be done [surrender to His will] on earth as it is in heaven give us this day our daily bread and forgive us our trespasses [debts] as we forgive those who trespass [debtors] against us, but lead us not into temptation, but deliver us from evil for Thine is the kingdom and the power and the glory forever. Amen. [Matthews 6:9-13]

Fear can drive so many decisions in our life. In fact, we give more power to the operation of fear than we give to the operation of love. If we fear something, we respect that fear and let it work in us and of us. However, with love we seem to allow love to take a back seat to fear. God has not given the spirit of fear, nor has He authorized us to use fear to manipulate one another. What He has given us is power, love and a sound mind! Don't be an agent for fear, don't let it rob you.

If we could get this in our spirit, tuck it in and hold fast to the truth about love. If we could remember this particular truth, life would be so much better. If we would allow perfect love to abide, in and of us and if we could approach all things with the spirit of true love we would be so much stronger and far more powerful in our walk. The power of love is unbeatable. Above all, love each other deeply, because love covers a multitude of sins. [I Peter 4:8] Love is so important and is often the only antidote or cure for a problem. If we had no love we would be ripped apart from one another because we are usually undeserving because of sin. God loves us beyond our short falls. The Word says that all have sinned and fall short of the glory of God, [Romans 3:23] God is aware that it is the nature of our flesh to pull away from the spirit, from life. However, God loves us deeply and perfectly. He loves us enough that we might have life. Imagine if He didn't, we would not be here now reading this book.

CHAPTER 22

Let it Go

When things are hard in life and we can't seem to handle them on our own, we either get resourceful or we fall apart. When I say resourceful, I mean we get creative with what it takes to achieve the goal. That may mean seeking help or guidance from others, pooling resources together to meet the need, or consulting an expert. The challenge here is that some things can't be solved with our own might. "For my thoughts are not your thoughts, neither are your ways my ways, saith the Lord." [Isaiah 55:8]

There are things that require far broader shoulders, greater wisdom, a more comforting bosom with an endless capacity to heal. God wants us to depend on Him for all of our concerns, even the little ones. "Trust in the Lord with all thine heart; and lean not unto thine own understanding." [Proverbs 3:5] When we look to Him spiritually, without our knowing, He is guiding us naturally. We can count on Him to see us through. You see when the spirit man stands, the natural man reclines. However, when we walk in the spirit, we are made wise in our surrendered disposition. Letting go, sounds like a cop out to some, but when we release our troubles to God we are acting in faith and wisdom. It is the intelligent approach to peaceful and blissful living.

Parable of the Unmerciful Servant found in Matthew 18: 21-35:

> Then Peter came to Jesus and asked, "Lord, how many times shall I forgive my brother when he sins against me? Up to seven times?"
>
> Jesus answered, "I tell you, not seven times, but seventy-seven times.
>
> "Therefore, the kingdom of heaven is like a king who wanted to settle accounts with his servants.
>
> As he began the settlement, a man who owed him ten thousand talents was brought to him.
>
> Since he was not able to pay, the master ordered that he and his wife and his children and all that he had be sold to repay the debt.
>
> "The servant fell on his knees before him. 'Be patient with me,' he begged, 'and I will pay back everything.' The servant's master took pity on him, canceled the debt and let him go.
>
> But when that servant went out, he found one of his fellow servants who owed him a hundred denarii. He

grabbed him and began to choke him. 'Pay back what you owe me!' he demanded.

His fellow servant fell to his knees and begged him, 'Be patient with me, and I will pay you back.'

But he refused. Instead, he went off and had the man thrown into prison until he could pay the debt.

When the other servants saw what had happened, they were greatly distressed and went and told their master everything that had happened.

Then the master called the servant in. 'You wicked servant,' he said, 'I canceled all that debt of yours because you begged me to.

Shouldn't you have had mercy on your fellow servant just as I had on you?'

In anger his master turned him over to the jailers to be tortured, until he should pay back all he owed.

"This is how my heavenly Father will treat each of you unless you forgive your brother from your heart."

There is a time for everything, and a season for every activity under heaven: a time to be born and a time to die, a time to plant and a time to uproot, a time to kill and a time to heal, a time to tear down and a time to build, a time to weep and a time to laugh, a time to tear and a *time to mend*. He has also set eternity in the hearts of men; yet they cannot fathom what God has done from beginning to end. I know that there is nothing better for men than to be happy and do good while they live. That everyone may eat and drink, and find satis-faction in all his toil—this is the gift of God. I know that everything God does will endure forever; nothing can be added to it and nothing taken from it. God does it so that men will revere him.

OBEDIENCE IS BETTER THAN SACRIFICE

"For rebellion is as the sin of witchcraft, and stubbornness is as iniquity and idolatry. Because thou hast rejected the word of the Lord, he hath also rejected thee from being king." [1Samuel 15:23]

Do your self a **BIG** favor....Let it Go

"Be kind to one another, *tender-hearted,* forgiving each other, just as God in Christ also has forgiven you." [Ephesians 4:32] It will never cease to amaze me how people go day after day purposing not to forgive. But these begrudging hearts cannot hide from God, no matter how often they go to church. God certainly does know your heart, even if it is hardened and incapable of true love. We all sin and fall short in areas of our life but we must diligently seek Him and seek His desire for our lives. There is no way in the world you can hold a grudge in one area and be pure in heart in another.

This section was one of the most difficult section for me to write because, I knew I had some areas that I needed to address, even if I felt innocent or otherwise. God is calling us to a higher commit-ment, where obedience is far better than sacrifice. God said forgive so you can be forgiven. "For sin shall not have dominion over you: for ye are not under law, but under grace." [Romans 6:14]

How many times will God forgive? Endless times, in fact He will forgive us innumerable times. God's love *keeps no record of wrongs!* This does not mean that we are to take advantage and keep doing wrong: we are to strive to be like Christ. We are to obey His commandments, we are to apply His principles to our lives. We are to ask, seek, and knock. We are to love one another unconditionally. If we sin against our brother, or have an aught with our brother, we are to go to our brother and ask his forgiveness, just as we repent to God for our sins. "This is my commandment, That ye love one another, as I have loved you. Greater love hath no man than this, that a man lay down his life for his friends. [John 15:12].

Look today at marriage—people so willingly and expeditiously throw in the towel. No one wants to change and apply the Word of God to their lives and to their marriages. If you commit your life and your marriage unto God, it will come under perfect submission. Well your relationship needs to be of one accord, and equally yoked and earnestly seeking answers from God. This marriage, your marriage brings glory to God. When you abuse your marriage because you take it in your own natural hands, rather than allowing the spirit of love to embrace your promises before God and before man, you bring damnation into your union. Give it to God and pray:

> *Father God, forgive me for my transgressions and give ear to my prayer dear Lord. I embrace your perfect gift of love. Father I call on your spirit to fill my heart until it overflows with your love and your delight. Father, forgive me for being full of myself and acting out of a controlling spirit and a judgmental spirit. I can not do anything without You. Please guide me. I pray dear Lord that your grace and tender mercies be with me always. Please anchor me in the power called love, that I may*

not walk in un-forgiveness and that I may not be grudg-ingly toward my brother. Lord, allow me to walk in the freedom and expression of love. Give me a new song and siege my tongue of words that kill. I want to talk out of love and impart love, speaking life into dead situations. Help me to love unconditionally seeking to encourage others and build them up. I repent of my sins yesterday, today and forever, Father God. I accept Your will for my life and I love you and want to love just like you. In Jesus name, Amen

We have not, because we ask not! Jesus says, "Ask, and it shall be given you, seek and you shall find, knock and it shall be opened to you. For everyone who asks receives, and he who seeks finds, and to him who knocks it shall be opened" [Matthew 7:7.8] How nice is it that God allows us to come to His grace boldly to obtain mercy and find grace. We can tap into his grace and mercy in times of need. In spite of our short falls, we are invited in. He has forgiven us because we asked and we seek and knock on the door of promise. In order to be forgiven, we must also be willing to forgive.

Hear this...*Love thinks no evil!* If we are not able to forgive, we are not able to love. If we have not love, we have nothing, we are nothing. In relationships we refer to this as blind love. This is truly God's way. When we fault find and blame, we are ignoring the principle of love. This is not to say that you should subject yourself to abuse or danger or toxic situations, but we must attempt to approach all matters in a manner that is pleasing to God. We are created in God's image and we need God's guidance. This way love prevails and we are free. We too, are free to approach the throne of grace.

This is a beautiful promise from God. "He who comes to me I will not at all cast out." [John 6:37] This is great, when it applies to us. When we can see that God is covering our faults with His unwavering love, it's a great benefit. God is all seeing and all knowing. He wants to wipe the canvas of our disobedience clean. We can't play the victim, the judge and the jury; instead we have to give all our cares over to Him and allow Him to sort things out for us. Yes, you may be hurt and you may even desire to get even but God wants you to trust Him and be confident in His supreme capabilities. We can not micro manage God or "His" people. We must let God be God!

You may find that your attempt to heal brokeness and confront a wicked person; it may result in the ugliest of uglies. That's okay, too. The word states many are the afflictions of the righteous, but God delivers us from them all. It takes a mighty mature, content and secure individual to love a person in spite of spewed pursecution. Know that in several instances the person that you have a hard time forgiving is often guilty and often innocent. You see, sometimes we cook things up in our carnal minds and make them bigger than they are. You have the tools to overcome much of this negative energy. If a snake bites you, you don't become a snake to bite back, you kill the snake with love. We have to strengthen the power of "positive thinking" to make the change first in the inward man, so that we see beautiful images and rehearse marvelous thoughts so that we can walk in the love God is calling us to. You are called to be willing, able and ready to forgive, love and trust God to work things out together for the good of those who love Him and are called according to His will. Harboring ill will and ill feelings hurts the one that refuses to let go and let God. It can cause all kinds of trouble, even sickness. Be reminded where the mind *goes* the body *follows!* This is detrimentally true as well as supernaturally true, depending where your head is at.

In order to forgive, you have to activate faith, hope and love. When you begin to move and groove in the rhythm of these gifts you will be better able to make a true committed transition in this area of your life. It is something you prupose in your heart and meditate on spiritually. You can change things in your thoughts which change the fruits of your lips into sweet words rather than bitter spews. The Jesus in you that ministers to the needs of His people. This can be your reality, but you must remove the stumbling blocks and simply forgive. Read aloud this prayer:

> *Father I love you and I know you love me. Help me to just Let it go! Help me to release past hurts, fears and entangled emotions. Create in me a clean heart and a clean mind. Lord give me a teachable spirit and a pliable heart. Lord hear my cry, I am sorry for being stubborn, resentful, prideful, judgemental and controlling. Lord I surrender all and I cry out yes to your will and your way. I have harbored and created a mountain of unforgiveness along the way and I want to be free right now, today. Lord please carve away the hardened areas in my life and make tender my heart Lord. Give me the power to rise in love and give it freely Lord. I want to love everyone and even my enemies Lord. Please teach me how to forgive and forget. Help me to move on so that I may heal this house, my body, mind and spirit. Lord I call out [call out those names the ones you have not forgiven] individually and I speak to hills protesting my love in You for them.*

Lord I want to be free and I want this to go down on the record as genuine. Truly pierce my heart and ready me to walk in true love. Counselor you are wonderous and magnificent and I adore you. Lord teach me, I want to learn how to love. We have been made in His likeness and now have been filled with His Spirit. We can now be available for God to use us for His Glory in bringing his light into this World. Amen.

What God makes clean is clean and what He makes whole is whole. What He sanctifies is sanctified and what He makes Holy is Holy. Where God marks righteousness is righteousness. Are you hearing me. When you give it over to God it belongs to Him. It is no longer yours, unless you pick it back up again. Going back into the same sin again and again is like a dog going back onto his own vomit. Rebuke that sin and turnaway from it. Refute it. Resist it and it will flee. God's Word is true and never void. Forgiving yourself is very hard to do, but you must learn to let IT go! Don't make the dangerous mistake of being angry with God. In all that He does, he has a good and perfect plan. Trust Him and only believe. It is your faith that gets His attention. You can have all confidence in God!

It was already documented that there would be a day where daughters and mothers, fathers and sons, siblings and loved ones would be at war with one another. Today we see alarming episodes of this reality. If we are expected to love our enemies, what more should be expected of us concerning our own flesh and blood or loved ones. There has to be unity, not division. God's vision is that of harmony and peace through love, not death! A house divided against itself can not stand. Tap into the gift of love inside of yourself and fix that which is broken. No matter how long ago, we must forgive and forget. We need one another more than we realize. Send a text message, email, or love letter—just do something to release the favor of God and benefit from His amazing grace and tender mercies. After all, obedience is better than sacrifice!

> *No man hath seen God at any time. If we love one another, God dwelleth in us, and his love is perfected in us. Hereby know we that we dwell in him, and he in us, because he hath given us of his Spirit. Herein is our love made perfect, that we may have boldness in the day of judgment: because as he is, so are we in this world. There is no fear in love; but perfect love casteth out fear: because fear hath torment. He that feareth is not made perfect in love. [1 John 4:12-18]*

Do your self a **BIG** favor; Don't be afraid to...Let it go.

CHATER 23

Push

Prepare to do the will of the Lord no matter how difficult the journey. You may not understand anything in your natural mind concerning the plans that God has for you, but through your obedience He will build you up and make wise your spirit man. The important thing to do is to remain steadfast and confident in knowing that God is ultimately in control of your life and He has your best interest at heart!

~PRAY UNTIL SOMETHING HAPPENS~

"Thou makest him to have dominion over the works of thy hands; Thou hast put all things under his feet." [Psalm 8:6] It's really not a secret, we are the children of the most-high God, and he sees us as special! He esteems us as the apple of His eye. He made us and saw that it was good. He did not make us computer programs but he made us living flesh with mind, body and soul. He gave us the freedom of choice so that we would continually choose Him of our own free will. He so loved us that He gave His ONLY begotten son, and whosoever believes in Him shall not perish but have everlasting life. The price was high and the price was paid for you and for me. Don't slumber, we ought to magnify Him!

There is nothing new under the sun. There is no thing new under The Son, The Messiah! God is the maker and creator of all things. He created you with a free will. However, you should know that when your will wars opposite His will, against His holiness, you lose power on every level. You need power now more than ever. Learn to respect the power of love. There is no time for foolishness or immaturity in the things of God. Seek a true relationship, so that you can hear from the Father and know His voice.

Allow the power of love to overwhelm you on the receiving and giving end. Let it rain love! Let it come down, "let it shower your soul and let the drops just penetrate you." [Leslie Oliver aka Jazmina] This writer and songstress bellowed, "I want to get happy in the rain, you ought to get happy in the rain, we better get happy in the rain, everybody get happy in the rain." The love and peace of God may not make since in the natural but it is a sure act of faith. Through active faith, you will move mountains. A woman of God, Evangelist Denise Bayes, once ministered that the dark is not such a bad thing. She referenced that it was in the dark that God created all things. This is a mind blower, for me. God did all this great work in the dark. The light injects the natural world, you begin to act by sight rather than by faith. In darkness, you must have faith, the substance of things hoped for and the evidence of things not seen. You can't see in the dark and God knows this, so when you are there, you can accomplish so much more by faith. Have faith and at the end of the storm, you'll see the golden sky. Speak light and life and have faith. You will rise!

When I think about my valley experiences, my low periods, episodes of darkness, I can zero in on the exact emotion I felt during that time frame. I felt defeated, abandoned, betrayed, alone, broken, hopeless. The doom and gloom had certainly set in. I have struggled through many events in my life some financial, some health, some career, some family, some this and some that. Usually I felt alone and isolated in my distress; and I felt like it was the end of the world. We often magnify our issues instead of looking to the Word.

I remember I entered a drawing for a huge prize. The first nine names selected would win a brand new house. Out of five-hundred-and-ninety-eight participants I was number five-hundred-and-ninety-eight. I giggled in disappointment, "It figures," I sighed. "I am always last and I should not expect anything else." I wondered why this trend always seemed to happen to me. Now I understand: it's because I speak it to life, I reinforce it, and (most dangerously) believe it! I was operating in failing faith rather than winning faith. I shared this with Minister Battle and she said, "Those who are last shall be first." If God said it I believe it. I instantly felt a confidence in knowing that my day would come in God's time and within His infinite wisdom. Just like the others that benefited from the lottery for new homes, I too would be blessed because God would not ever forsake me.

It is how we look at things that either fuels us or drains us. That is why God has given us the Word, to apply it to every area of our lives. God wants us to exercise Faith so He can move on to building us up in other areas of our lives. Get past the doubting zone; move into a place where even when opposition strikes stand firm in knowing that Jesus Christ is Lord. With that being true every knee shall bow and every tongue confess He is Lord.

Over the years I have heard many great stories. Many things will make nearly perfect sense to us, such as commandments and so on. However there will be things that are not clear at all. Most imperatively we have to learn that obedience really is better than sacrifice. When we can obey God period, we will be better off. The following story, for which the author is unknown, provides insight into the move of God and our call to obedience.

A man was sleeping at night in his cabin when suddenly his room filled with bright light and the Savior appeared. The Lord told the man He had work for him to do, and showed him a large rock in front of his cabin. The Lord explained that the man was to push against the rock with all his might. This, the man did, day after day.

For many years he toiled from sun up to sun down with his shoulders set squarely against the cold, massive surface of the unmoving rock, pushing with all his might. Each night the man returned to his cabin sore, and worn out, feeling that his whole day had been spent in vain.

Seeing that the man was showing signs of discouragement, the Adversary decided to enter the picture by placing thoughts into the man's weary mind: "You've been pushing against that rock for a long time, and it hasn't budged. Why kill yourself over this? You're never going to move it." This gave the man the impression that the task was impossible and that he was a failure. These thoughts discouraged and disheartened the man.

"Why kill myself over this?" He thought. "I'll just put in my time, giving just the minimum effort. That'll be good enough." And that's just what he planned to do— until one day he decided to make it a matter of prayer and take his troubled thoughts to the Lord.

"Lord," he said, "I've labored long and hard in Your service, putting all my strength to do that which You've asked. Yet, after all this time, I haven't even budged that rock by half a millimeter. What's wrong? Why am I failing?"

The Lord responded compassionately,

"My friend, when I asked you to serve Me— you accepted. I told you that your task was to push against the rock with all your strength— which you've done. Never once did I mention to you that I expected you to move it. Your task was to push. And now you come to Me— with your strength spent, thinking that you've failed. But is that really so?"

"Look at yourself. Your arms are strong and muscular. Your back sinew is mighty. Your hands are callused from the constant pressure; and your legs have become massive and hard. Through opposition you've grown

241

much and your abilities now surpass that which you used to have. Yet you haven't moved the rock. But your calling was to be obedient and to push and to exercise your faith and trust in My wisdom. This you've done. I, my friend, will now move the rock."

Pushing that rock was not such a bad idea. The rock may have been literally a rock, but in your life think of the things that the rock may represent. You may be tired, frustrated and bordering doubt, if you are not there already, but you must stand and keep pushing. Get in position and pray that rock out of your way. Pray that mountainous event away and trust God to literally move on your behalf. Change is going to come.

CHAPTER 24

Joy

IN THY PRESENCE IS FULLNESS OF JOY; AT THY
RIGHT HAND ARE PLEASURES FOREVER MORE.
[PSALMS 16:11]

RESTORE UNTO ME THE JOY OF THOU SALVATION
AND UPHOLD ME WITH THY FREE SPIRIT.
[PSALMS 51:12]

NOW THE LORD IS THAT SPIRIT: AND WHERE THE
SPIRIT OF THE LORD IS, THERE IS LIBERTY.
[2 CORINTHIANS 3:17]

THEY THAT SOW IN TEARS SHALL REAP IN JOY.
[PSALMS 126:5]

In the presence of something greater than yourself, you will learn great things. If we are the temple of God, and God abides in us, then we must submit our will unto God. He is greater than we are. The scripture says that "the spirit of a man will sustain him in his infirmity, but as for a wounded spirit, who can bare it?" [Proverbs 18:14] Joy is a choice, as is life eternal! Recognizing the good in every situation is easier when you discover that "The **joy** of the Lord is your strength." [Nehemiah 8:10] Even when it hurts and doubt has cast a cloud before us, we must hold onto the promises of the Father.

> *To appoint unto them that mourn in Zion, to give unto them beauty for ashes, the oil of joy for mourning, the garment of praise for the spirit of heaviness; that they might be called trees of righteousness, the planting of the Lord, that he might be glorified.* [Isaiah 61:3]

In life we have options, choices and decisions to make. What a privilege! When God created us with free will, we automatically became privy to options, choices and decisions. Needless to say some will be wise, while others may be plain foolish.

Most people are joyful when they have what they want, but this joy is short lived; we always seem to want more and more and more. When we are unable to have what we want as fast as we want it, we tend to lose our joy or sense of satisfaction. What is joy anyway? The dictionary might say that it is a state of an emotion bringing about feelings of great happiness or pleasure, especially of an elevated spiritual kind. When we think of joy and its origin, we might ponder on the truth that joy comes from within. How do you tap into joy, that which is within?

Let's agree that joy is an emotion. Emotions are used to describe the state of a person. It gives a title to a persons disposition or countenance. Joy is an emotion, just as happiness, sadness, loneliness, fear, anger, love, hate, sorrow, disgust, acceptance, anticipation, surprise, jealousy and envy are all emotions that affect us both internally and externally. As I always say, *where the mind goes, the body follows.* As your emotional countenance takes position of your inner man, it shows up in the face of your outward man through expressions and behaviors.

If your joy is *linked* to things, you can look forward to an emotional roller coaster: A life of temporary highs and plunging lows, because no thing will last forever. Every person, place and thing has a guarantee... a guarantee that it will become old, or broken by the woes of life. See what I mean by plunging lows? It is a painful reality that keeps us chasing false hope and setting ourselves up for *face* value rather than *faith* value. Why place such value in the things that bring about false joy and endless letdowns? Perhaps, just maybe, we should reshape our desires and long for the things that bring about true joy and real love. The Word of God says in Psalms 37:4 "delight thyself in the Lord; and he shall give thee the desires of thine heart." He is talking about the desires of the indwelling heart, the heart of the indwelling spirit, in other words the heart of the Holy One. If God is one with us, then the desires that bring us true delight will be consistent with His perfect will. We will find joy and peace and abundance and eternal life.

When we long for material gain more than we long for eternal gain, we get lost in the emptiness of temporary joy. This leads to hurt and disappointment. We can't live through life with our hands out, constantly waiting to receive. To experience joy when you are receiving something is easy, but the joy that comes from giving is better, more fulfilling. God blesses the cheerful giver. The only way to experience unfailing joy and love is to seek God and to please Him. In doing so, he bestows peace that surpasses all understanding. He gives you another perspective on all things. His Holy Spirit teaches you how to view things through His eyes. You learn to look at all things through love as you walk in harmony with His spirit. Joy was admirably spoken by writer Elizabeth B. Brown who titled her work *Joy Choice: Happiness Is an Inside Job.* Happiness certainly is an inside job. It is the inner works of the Lord that fulfills us with the harmony needed to keep joy and peace. We want to be able to view things in perfection—the only way to do that is to have the love and heart of Christ. Change your mind and change your heart and talk to Him daily. He will mold you into a vessel of Joy and as other's see the new birth in you they will be drawn by the decision you made. You will be glad you did.

> *In thy name shall they rejoice all the day: and in thy righteousness shall they be exalted. [Psalms 89:16], But let the righteous be glad; let them rejoice before God: yea, let them exceedingly rejoice. [Psalms 68:3], But let all those that put their trust in thee rejoice: let them ever shout for joy, because thou defendest them: let them also that love thy name be joyful in thee. [Psalms 5:11], Therefore my heart is glad, and my glory rejoiceth: my flesh also shall rest in hope. [Psalms 16:9], For his anger endureth but a moment; in his favour is life: weeping may endure for a night, but joy cometh in the morning. [Psalms 30:5], And my soul shall be joyful in the Lord: it shall rejoice in his salvation. [Psalms 35:9], Then will I go unto the altar of God, unto God my exceeding joy: yea, upon the harp will I praise thee, O God my God. [Psalms 43:4],*

Now thanks be unto God, which always causeth us to triumph in Christ, and maketh manifest the savour of his knowledge by us in every place. [2 Corinthians 2:14], As also ye have acknowledged us in part, that we are your rejoicing, even as ye also are ours in the day of the Lord Jesus. [2 Corinthians 1:14]

Sing, O heavens; and be joyful, O earth; and break forth into singing, O mountains: for the Lord hath comforted his people, and will have mercy upon his afflicted [Isaiah 49:13], 7Even them will I bring to my holy mountain, and make them joyful in my house of prayer: their burnt offerings and their sacrifices shall be accepted upon mine altar; for mine house shall be called an house of prayer for all people. [Isaiah 56:7], And the ransomed of the Lord shall return, and come to Zion with songs and everlasting joy upon their heads: they shall obtain joy and gladness, and sorrow and sighing shall flee away. [Isaiah 35:10]

CHAPTER 25

Quiet Waters

Our attitudes toward what we weather have a vibrant impact on how we come out of each situation. God being the author and finisher of our fate has overall control of all matters. However He gave us, a very unique and special gift called free will. That will is what allows us room to pick and choose through out this lifetime, which way we desire to go. Our choices result in either setbacks or set-ups. It is His perfect love that allows us repeated failed attempts to get things right. When you are connected to Christ your encounters with opposition are different from when you are not. Staying on the path to righteousness is best maintained with a ready, willing, and obedient vessel. He will lead you along the stillness of quiet waters as you journey through your valley experiences. A peaceful spirit is a quiet spirit. Do not allow people or things to make toxic your spirit. If you love the Lord, you will be tried. But when you do, remember that silence is golden, the Lord will speak for you—perhaps through you—but you must be wise. Never allow the daughters and sons of darkness to get you on board with them. Instead remain quiet, meek, calm and humble. Quiet strength is strength indeed! Don't worry God is in control. I pray that you are drawn near to Him.

There is nothing like the sanctification of tranquility. Today we live in very stressful times. Life has become so difficult to manage that it robs us of time and space, stealing our joy and serenity. Peace is the one thing that is free of charge. Even though God offers the kind of peace that can quench any storm with calmness, surpassing reasonable consideration, we don't settle down long enough to dwell in the essence of God given peace. In fact in today's times, people are going out of their way to recreate peace, and they are spending big money to grasp peace. People go to day spas, meditation classes, breathing classes, scream lounges, you name it, to capture some level of calm. But these things could never measure up to what God offers us. Peace should abide in you. We can ensure a serene environment by not losing control of our reactions to the changing tides of our life. God is our blessed assurance that all is well. We rest in the confidence of knowing that He alone can speak to the wind and have it obey.

It is difficult to rely on the kind of peace that is fashioned by the hands of man. If you find yourself in chaos, it is safe to say that you may need to take personal inventory of why you've lost control. Once you have done this, make the necessary adjustments to clean house, so to speak. Then God can usher in the sweetness of tranquil living. Don't beat yourself down for your mistakes—we are all human and we all err at times. Error is a wonderful learning vehicle, taking you out of the slumps of sin into the slopes of greatness. Through trial-and-error you become wise and fit for tumultuous times. Faith and peace go hand in hand. When your faith fails, your peace becomes distant.

In life there are events that will make you wonder how you are still breathing in the midst of the storm, because it hurts so badly. I can name a few events where I felt this way: when I lost my mother, when one of my closest friends was murdered, when I was betrayed by someone I trusted, and when I was visited by severe illness. I remember being so upset that breathing literally was a challenge and victory all at once. I could not pull myself together because I was focusing on the problem, giving it life through a defeated countenance. Through God, the answer to every problem can be found. During my storms, I distinctly remember asking God to grant me peace, the kind that surpasses all understanding. Instantly, I experienced calm. At that point I had given up. I know it didn't happen until I got still enough to embrace it. In my surrender, God captured me and began to work things out. God will show you who He is and all you need to do is believe and trust Him.

In Part I of this inspiration, I shared some of the storms I had encountered personally. Storms can come to bring pain and leave devastation. Dealing with the aftermath of these storms can feel impossible. You may be in the center of a storm wondering if and when it will ever end. Your question may even lead you to doubt that survival is possible. In such fear and doubt, I in confidence remind you that there is no such thing as an eternal storm. Storms have to obey God, remember that. Focus on the light at the end of the tunnel. While storm's bring devastation, the healing process brings deliverance and restoration. Often during the phase of recovery one taps into uncharted strength, and is far more capable than imagined, respective to what one can and cannot bare.

No one is exempt from such painful trials and so we must, each passing day, develop and make strong our spirit. Not that you are ready for such trials, but more importantly connected to the one who is. No matter what we do, when the wind is knocked out of us, we can anticipate discomfort, but rely on the strength of the Father. Be still and be silent so you can hear what the Lord is saying. You must allow yourself the time and space to freely experience the perfect Love that only God can offer.

No matter what the wind brings and how intense the struggle becomes, we must remain focused and confident in God. "Do not therefore, abandon that confidence of yours; it brings a great reward." [Hebrews 10:35] "Be assured and do not lose your fearlessness nor cast away your boldness, but rest in the comfort of knowing that all things work together for the good of those who love God, and who are called according to his plan." [Romans 8:28]

In some instances, a storm is comparable to walking through the valley—it can be compared to the shadow of death. But in the twenty-third Psalm, the psalmist assumes a posture of "in spite of:" In spite of darkness and uncertainty, I will stand on this Rock of salvation fully aware that I may be down but not dead, rocked but not ruined, through the storms tossed and turned but not taken out or finished. It is miraculous what God can do with you in the storm, through the storm and after the storm. He is always there, as a present help in times of trouble. Remember God said the afflictions would be many, and in the same breath He promised to deliver you from them all. Although the tranquil indulgences of man can be very instrumental, nothing can compare to the true peace that dwells within the mind and spirit of the man who has opted to place all his trust in God.

Psalm 23

The Lord is my shepherd, I shall not be in want.

He makes me lie down in green pastures, He leads me beside quiet waters,

He Restores my soul. He guides me in paths of righteousness for his name's sake. Even though I walk through the valley of the shadow of death, I will fear no evil, for you are with me; your rod and your staff, they comfort me.

You prepare a table before me in the presence of my enemies. You anoint my head with oil; my cup overflows. Surely goodness and love will follow me all the days of my life, and I will dwell in the house of the Lord forever.

The 23rd Psalm of David is one of the first Psalms I learned as a small child. Anytime there was trouble at home, my Mother would tell us to read the 23rd Psalm over and over out loud. I noticed that this particular inspiration provided peace, internal peace. I say internal because it comes from God. There is a difference between internal peace and the external peace of the world—internal peace is something you can count on, something which won't leave you.

If you look at David's life, you can't help but see the many trials he went through including the numbered attempts on his life. What lies in your wilderness? Would you complain or do something about it? David was first a shepherd in the wilderness; later in life, a different set of circumstances drove him to the wilderness. It was David's faith and attitude that kept him.

There is a song by the late Bishop William C. Abney called "I Won't Complain." In this song the writer shares the emotions of those who feel broken. Sing with me…

I've had some good days, I've had some hills to climb

I've had some weary days, and some sleepless nights

But when I look around, and I think things over

All of my good days, outweigh my bad days, and I won't complain

Sometimes the clouds hang low, I can hardly see the road

I ask a question Lord, Why so much pain?

But He knows what's best for me,
Although my weary eyes, they can't see

So I'll just say, Thank You Lord, I won't complain

The Lord has been so good to me, He's been so good to me,

More than this old world or you could ever be, He's been so good to me

He dried all of my tears away, turned my midnights into day

So I'll just say Thank You Lord, And I won't complain.

The writer confesses that in spite of the storms, God can roll back the clouds—He knows what is best for us. The lyrics express the emotion following an event of circumstances overtook the speaker. It matters not what the circumstances were, because God is intimately connected to our troubles. Trouble could be more debts than money, an ending relationship, sickness in the body, spiritual brokenness, rebellion, a stolen vehicle, or the loss of a loved one.

There is a way to address these burdens so that they don't consume you completely. Typically when you focus on an issue, you focus on the problem instead of the solution. The solution is in Christ. When we go about things ourselves, no one has our backs. Here is what Psalm 55:22 offers: "Cast thy burden upon the Lord, and he shall sustain thee: he shall never suffer the righteous to be moved." I don't know about you, but for me, when I read the book of Psalms, I experience a hearty exhale. The Psalms are comforting, offering poetic enlightenment. They share with us David's walk with the Lord, his encounters with opposition, his encouragements to us. Furthermore, they offer protective prayers that address any issue you could imagine. David was a worshipper! He was masterful at praising the Lord. When the rages of your storm seem to be more than you can handle, lose yourself in praise.

It is comforting to know that trouble won't last always and we will wind up victorious, regardless. This alone gives me a sense of peace. God has ordained His word as total truth. Therefore when we speak His word in faith, it prospers us. When God leads us vehemently beside still waters, He is purposing a peaceful pursuit. He is leading us and guiding us along the path of tranquility. When we veer off we find ourselves in situations that are often beyond our know-how. If we would simply stay in His arms, we would be protected and comforted. Wisdom will make a gospel seeker of you; in the pursuit of peace you will seek a true relationship with your creator.

CHAPTER 26

Walking in Authority of Love

HOW DO WE WALK IN AUTHORITY? FIND OUT WHO YOU ARE.

WHEN DO WE WALK IN AUTHORITY? FIND OUT WHOSE YOU ARE.

WHAT DO WE DO WHEN WE ARE FINALLY THERE? TAKE IT BY FORCE.

Maintain your authority as descendents of Christ… Forget about the past, keep the faith, walk in love, and seek a relationship with your Creator. Without FAITH, it is impossible to please God. To be close to Christ we must walk in love. Without LOVE, there is no relationship. Without RELATIONSHIP, there is no walk. If there is no walk, there is no power. POWER goes hand in hand with authority. Once you are AUTHORIZED, you are a problem and you become a threat to your enemy.

> *But his delight is in the law of the Lord, and on his law he mediates day and night. He is like a tree planted by streams of water, which yields its fruit in season and whose leaf does not wither. Whatever he does prospers.* (Psalms 1:2, 3)

It does not matter who you are, where you are, what you've done, or where you've been, God can and will use you towards His glory, for which you were created to celebrate. Bump what the devils say; God said you are His prize possession. You belong to Him!

> *May He strengthen your hearts so that you will be blameless and holy in the presence of our God and Father when our Lord Jesus comes with all his holy ones.* [1 Thessalonians 3:13]

I hope the authenticity of my story can and has helped you. At the age of nineteen, I watched my closest friend die in the street, a defenseless teenager. By the age of twenty I dropped out of college, too much to bare. At twenty-one I was pregnant and married. At twenty-four I was involved with a married man, selfish and foolish. By twenty-six I had his daughter. Yet when I turned twenty-seven I gave my life to the Lord, and by thirty I was divorced and remarried. For many reasons I felt undeserving of good things and I felt like I shouldn't have a voice, that is a public voice. But God continued to tug and usher, tug and usher and I could not help but answer and go, answer and go. I made mistakes, big ones at that. I want you to know that no matter "what it was," no devil can stop "what it is." You belong to a loving, forgiving and establishing God. The deeper the pit; the greater the glory. No matter how big the hole is that you have dug for yourself, God will restore you and make you whole. No matter what "they" say, hear what God has to say about you.

Here are some selections from Isaiah Chapter 54:

> *...Fear not, for you will not be put to shame; and do not feel humiliated, for you will not be disgraced; But you will forget the shame of your youth, and the reproach of your widowhood you will remember no more... For a brief moment I forsook you, but with great compassion I will gather you. In an outburst of anger I hid My face from you for a moment, but with everlasting loving kindness I will have compassion on you...For the mountains may be removed and the hills may shake, but My loving kindness will not be removed from you, and My covenant of peace will not be shaken. O afflicted one, storm-tossed, and not comforted. Behold, I will set your stones in antimony, and your foundations I will lay in sapphires. Moreover, I will make your battlements of rubies, and your gates of crystal, and your entire wall of precious stones. All your sons will be taught of the Lord; and the well-being of your sons will be great. In righteousness you will be established; you will be far from oppression, for you will not fear; and from terror, for it will not come near you. If anyone fiercely assails you it will not be from Me. Whoever assails you will fall because of you. Behold, I Myself have created the smith who blows the fire of coals and brings out a weapon for its work; and I have created the destroyer to ruin. No weapon that is formed against you will prosper; And every tongue that*

accuses you in judgment you will condemn. This is the heritage of the servants of the Lord, and their vindication is from Me.

Let's focus on love, walking away from all un-forgiveness, nurturing our relationship with the Father, and exercising repentance. You, through the power of love and piety, can move mountains because of your faith and the magnitude of your love. In the name of Jesus of Nazareth you will receive authorization from the heavens to work wonders here on earth. Perhaps you thought of the above scripture as mere words, or maybe you have this idea that it only applies to someone else, not you. But I will say this again: To you the reader and student of the gospel, believing through Christ you will "Heal the sick, raise the dead, cleanse the lepers, cast out demons: freely ye received, freely give." [Matthew 10:8]

It is your faith that will fight for you, not your might. It is your faith in God all the way and it is by your faith that actual healing and deliverance goes forth. Every knee shall bow to the name of Jesus! We refer to the adversary as the strong man, who comes to plague you and overthrow you. Without faith it is impossible to please God. We being servants have much work to do. In what we do, the goal is to do our jobs well, and to hear "Well done." Are you growing strong enough to believe in the Christ that is within you, rather than trusting in man? To whom much is given, much is required. What have you done for Him lately? God's word says, "I pray that your faith fail not." Don't fail God and disappoint Him. Work on your faith and then improve your works, for faith without works is dead.

Instead, with great vigor, get busy doing the will of God. Be victorious in Him; fight to save His children. We live on a spiritual battleground, all being soldiers in God's army. Every believer has been given the authority to walk in the power of God. You have the authority to walk in the power of the sons and daughters, of the most High God. If by faith we exercise the gifts within us, we can do all things through Christ who strengthens us. We have authority over sickness, demonic powers, situations and circumstances. We must change our way of thinking; from carnal to supernatural (see Romans 12:2).

Remember in the word of God, it says "greater things shall you do." There is life and death in the power of the tongue. "So shall my word be that goeth from out of my mouth; it shall not return unto me void, but it shall prosper in the thing whereto I sent it" Isaiah 55:11 (King James Version). You have the power and authority to pray and change things around you, so long as it is the will of God. This is why you must read scripture and gain knowledge of and power in the word of God. The more you eat the Bread of Life, the stronger you become.

I don't have to tell you that to approach strongholds you will need strength. I think you know this for yourself. But I am going to remind you that if you have not done the groundwork by preparing through consecration, fasting and praying coupled with faith, be still. Don't try if you are not ready. If you had to fight a professional boxer in the next six months, you would not go in that ring unprepared? No—you would get fit for that day with everything that is in you, so at the appointed hour you would have the confidence and strength you needed to stand a chance. In the spirit world you need to be spiritually fit, as well. Fully believe that with God before you and through the blood of Jesus, the adversary is already defeated. But you have to be a learned student of the gospel of Jesus Christ.

With God before you, no demon can stand against you. Jesus said, "If you hold to my teaching...Then you will know the truth, and the truth shall set you free." [John 8:31, 32]

You will be strengthened in the knowledge of God. "Man does not live by bread alone but on every word that comes from the mouth of God." [Matthew 4:4] In and through His word, there is a solution for you, for me, and for everyone. The word of God is our bread of life. It is the way, the only way. Everything that you are going through or have gone through is your testament and ministry. If the road was rough, I am certain that you were tougher than those rough roads. God will not give us more than we can bare. The enemy is hard at work trying to keep you from the knowledge of God and the truth about who you are in God. In Him, you are above a conqueror. You are chosen for great work. Know who you are, make your election sure. Tap into the power of God and stand on His Rock of Salvation—you will win because you are on the winning team. Delight yourself in the law of the Lord, and on His law, mediate day and night. He will nurture you like a tree planted by a gentle stream, which yields its fruit in season and whose leaves do not wither. Whatever you do will prosper.

CHAPTER 27

For You IV

IN THIS, THE FINAL CHAPTER OF MY BOOK,
I HAVE PROVIDED WORDS TO MEDITATE UPON
AND A JOURNAL TO RECORD YOUR PERSONAL,
SPIRITUAL EXPERIENCES.

EXERCISE

Purpose to surrender your will to the good and perfect will of the Lord. Exhale your thoughts, your will and your way. Now inhale His greatness and will. Ask for divine guidance concerning sensitivity in spirit and discernment for truth. Affirm that you will never walk alone. Go forward with the Christ that reigns victorious. Imagine you have dropped a ton of baggage and are now free from the shackles they embodied. Meditate on that which is good, pure and joyful. Know that your storms have been calmed, your fear has been engulfed in the flames of faith, love has pierced the heart of your spirit, and you are now captivated in the quietness of still waters. No longer are you a slave to the fear of the yesterdays or tomorrows: you have completely surrendered your weaknesses to the strength that only God can give. You have been anointed and appointed to walk in authority with Christ.

Record your thoughts here in letter format. Include areas where you may need extra focus and continued exercise. Start out by addressing this letter *"Abba Father."* Repent first, thank him and glorify him second, then write your love letter to God. Remember to be specific with your prayer petitions. Anticipate a breakthrough.

Record your love letter to God below:

_____

_____

_____

_____

_____

_____

_____

_____

_____

_____

_____

IN CLOSING

-Be ye transformed by the renewing of your mind-

As you reflect upon your experiences as I have, I pray full-heartedly that your faith fail not. I pray that you are enlightened and inspired to march on with unmovable assurance. There will be days when the blizzards of scornful accounts seem endless and the road grows dim, but we as sons and daughters of the Most High God must remember that faith is our platform and our promise. Even as we travel through the darkest valleys of our lives, we will be both guided and guarded. And even then we have the Word that gives light. Never forget that when you walk through your storm, stay focused and remain grounded only looking to the hills from whence cometh your strength and help. Should fear enter the picture, pray, press, push, prevail, be empowered and take your triumph by force.

> Let faith bridge the troubled waters and let Love lead both sons and daughters. May joy be your morning song and peace, kiss you all day long. May patience be your unspoken voice, as kindness is your daily choice. May goodness pierce your heart always as faith increases more each day. Be gentle with each and every soul; bestowed upon you, self control.

Be a Lion. [Proverbs. 28:1]

ABOUT THE AUTHOR

I greet you all in the spirit of victory as I am overjoyed to speak about the flower in my life, Sonya "Ruby" Ward. She is a devoted mother who can burn behind the stove. She is a visionary who can deliver eye opening ideas that stimulate untouched creativity in other's. She knows how to yield to the dreams of our children, incrementally releasing nugget's of wisdom and much needed support, while balancing life's demands. When asked about my wife's initial start in the field of writing, I must say that she's been writing for a long time. Every time the opportunity presents itself to encourage someone through a trial, she instantly start's to write. Now the finished product called, fear is NOT MY boss has culminated. The bible say's in psalm 45:1, "My tongue is the pen of a ready writer," and while speaking to the common anxieties of this life, that many of her friends and family shared, she stored the cause, the effect, and the solution to these problems in her mental rolodex. I am in awe of God's timing for this book and I am persuaded to believe that the seed that is being sown in the lives of its readers will also encourage the author when the inevitable nature of man rears its head. Ruby you have graduated with honors upon finishing this great work. It has ministered to me and I applaud you for your commitment and god given ingenuity.

Minister Cecil Bernard Ward
Faith Temple, East Orange, NJ

SONYA WARD

Born and raised in the township of Montclair, New Jersey, Sonya is one of five children born to the angelic Julia Marie Woods-Long, bless her soul and Alton Richard Long Senior of Greensboro, NC. It was her love for music that drew Sonya to the church as a small child; and at twelve she joined the choir and was baptized. Following her parent's separation, Sonya's family moved often, as a result she met Christians along the way who planted great seeds in her spirit. Though Sonya strayed during her teenage years and was not active in her call to service, the seeds were planted nonetheless. Through her early twenties she constantly gave of herself in service to help others, balancing her personal and professional life. After many set backs and personal storms, Sonya met and married EPIC singer, writer, and recording artist Cecil B. Ward, who would later walk in ministry. They are under the tutelage of Bishop Aaron L. Hobbs and Pastor Yvette Anderson of Faith Temple in East Orange, NJ.

Today Sonya is the devoted wife of Minister Cecil B. Ward and mother of four amazing children: Sonyae Elise, Naiani Charise, Silva Bernard and step-daughter Skye Ambrasai. Over the years she has been sharing her gift in service to uplift others as a friend and life coach in both professional and personal arenas. Sonya has been writing most of her life, in a broad array of expressions. She has written songs, poems, stories, career development tools, marketing and motivational tools and now her first book, Fear Is Not My Boss. In addition she has designed, implemented, and launched workshops/road shows for "It's Everything Beautiful" in a collaborative effort to touch the broken by planting seeds of faith. Sonya has also pioneered lunch-hour bible studies for small groups at major corporations. Sonya is a board member for Students of The Word (SOW) under the counsel and direction of Reverend Milton B. Hobbs.

OTHER MINISTRY INFORMATION

REV. MILTON B. HOBBS serves as Pastor of New Covenant Fellowship of Clark, New Jersey, Additionally he serves as Executive Director of Students of the Word, Inc a New Jersey non-profit capacity building and training organization. Professionally, he manages the Division of Community Development for the City of East Orange. He is married and the father of four children. Milton B. Hobbs

---

APRIL GREGORY (CPMC), Are you a Christian-prenuerer? Are you struggling to build your business? April's coaching style blends an inner-spiritual and outer-strategic approach yielding her clients an unfair advantage.

She has invoked the successes of many including multi-million dollar producing spas to individuals in the United States Marine Corps. Knowledgeable and passionate, April Gregory and her coaching group will unify their objectives with yours; in doing so creating a relationship that undeniably fosters success.

Contact April Gregory, *Marketing Consultant & Strategist* at:

www.AprilGregoryInc.com
AG Consulting Group
908-313-2225

INSPIRATION AND REFERENCE:

CHAPTER 10:
Merriam-Webster Online Dictionary © 2005
Merriam-Webster, Incorporated
Walking Into Your Destiny
Juanita Bynum, Charisma House 2004

CHAPTER 16:
Called to Greatness
Ron Hutchinson, Moody 2001

CHAPTER 19:
Praying the Names of God
Ann Spangler, Zondervan 2004

CHAPTER 26:
Take It by Force
Judy Jacobs, Charisma House

A VERY SPECIAL THANKS TO:

My dear uncle, Rev. Reginald McClain
Shiloh Baptist Church, Scranton, PA.

My friend, Rev. Ronald Paige
1st Baptist Church, Long Branch, NJ

My Father in law, Rev. Alfred Vincent Ward
Tampa Florida

THANK YOU TO:

Joi, April, Elder Ieisha, Lady Rose, Tracey, Mia, Charlotte, James, JoAnn,
Gena, Mother Ward, Rev. Ward, Elder Antonio, Vickie and Joel, Julia,
Howard, Richard, Marva, Zionette, Carol, Darlana, Fred, Bonnie, Kim,
Diane and Grantley, Susan, Robin and Amani.

Author of "The Secret Exposed"

Donna Matthews Aka *Lady Gido'rah*

I am the third generation to be born in a small town in Plainfield NJ. Born in February of 1961, I always liked to joke that I was born on the exact day and year as Lady Diana, though unfortunately, I would not live the life of a princess.

I studied religious education at Oakwood College. Learning about the things of God has been a lifetime quest for me. I suffered a difficult childhood and having a spiritual center has helped me to overcome my life issues. It has also propelled me to search for the answers and the secrets to life.

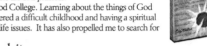

www.TheSecretExposedsite.com

Author of "Fear is Not My Boss"

Sonya R.Ward Author , "Empowerment Expert and Motivational Speaker" offers a compelling read in "Fear is Not My Boss" A true work of inspiration, Fear is No My Boss is a practical restorative easy read, food for the soul. It drives the desire to leap into purpose! The book was coined as one of the badest bullets you can reload with! Author Sonya R.Ward helps the reader to uproot the seeds of hindrance, move mountains and walk in the authority to form miracles by faith from the words we speak.

www.SonyaWard.com

Author of "The Trinity Collection"

Regina is the author of "Innocent Victims", "Take Care Of Your Credit", and "Good Credit Is No Secret". This talented young entrepreneur mom is slowly making history with her strong courage to speak and open the gateway for new leaders. She was nominated for Literary Blog and Publicist of the Year Award scheduled in 2010. She has been a featured quest on radio stations across the country and is gaining national attention. She writes for several newspapers across the country, writes in numerous magazines and is the Orlando Personal Finance Examiner. Her latest projects include "The Credit Digest Magazine", National Dons and Divas Credit Tour, CD God is Real, and Innocent Victims Show. For more information email her advocate102@hotmail.com 321-287-0986 www.reginalittles.com www.koxpublishing.com

www.ReginaLittles.com

Founder of " the Healing Empire"

My Love for Life and Service is a very fulfilling journey that gets better with time. In my minds' eye, I see the greatness that we all have been blessed with. Mentor, Dancer, Graphic Designer, Choreographer Anthony Harris: urbanvision@gmail.com

www.Da1kidsolo.com

Sonya Ward:

Author, Empowerment Expert, Motivational Speaker and Public Figure

Books:

Fear Is Not My Boss! *To Weather The Storm:* ISBN 978-0-615-23046-7

New Book Releases:

LEAP Mountains, Land Miracles! (Coming Soon)

Founder:

Miracles NOW Int'l Empowerment Ministries

Life Channels Empowerment Group Consulting Services

For Bookings:

Book Signings, Speaking Engagements, Evangelism, Vending and Special Events

Contact Us:

info@mylifechannels.com

unstoppableyou@att.net

Life Channels Empowerment Group

PO Box 1877, Montclair, NJ 07042

Operation L.E.A.P Inquiries,
Your High Impact Empowerment Experience
Leveraging Excellence and Total Prosperity
WWW.SONYAWARD.COM
INFO@MYLIFECHANNELS.COM

OPERATION "L.E.A.P"

Leveraging Excellence and Prosperity

Another Year Bites the Dust--

If you are ready to burn the bridges of procrastination, as it relates to your purpose, passion and position in life, today is the perfect day to L.E.A.P into Destiny, breaking the never ending cycle of being stuck-

> In the early 1500s the first orange tree was planted by early Spanish explorers later becoming one of the hottest commodities on the shelf. While the Orange in and of itself was awesome, the bursting brilliance of its juice became Awe-Tastic! Why? Because someone envisioned the excellence of a juicy orange on a hot summer day thus leveraging the kind of prosperity that positioned them for greatness (its benefits) and prosperity (its rewards).

So I have one question-- WHAT'S IN YOUR HANDS? What gifts, talents and skills are you taking for granted. News Flash; "Wealth is with YOU"

It's a pleasure to meet unstopABLE you, I'm Sonya Ward, Empowerment Expert, Author and Speaker. If you're ready to experience life in abundance of joy, excellence and total prosperity then there's no better time than now! Operation L.E.A.P will give you the tools and knowledge to move your dreams from vision to manifold blessings!

REGISTER Today for a LEAP Workshop, Conference or Affiliate Program

You will learn:

LEAP Mountains
How To Turn Opposition into Opportunity
How To Overcome The Barriers of Fear
How To Strengthen Your Countenance at The Eye of The Storm
How To Smash Sinking Thinking (Negative Cycling)
How To Bounce Back From A History of Hurts
LAND MIRACLES
How To Position Yourself For Total Prosperity
How To Penetrate Your Ordained Purpose
How To Become A Money Magnet Doing What You Love
How To Master The Power of Influence
How To Maximize Your Unique Value
How To Expand The Brand You
How To Become A Connector
How To Master Relationship Building
How To Manage and Maintain True Success

www.sonyaward.com/sonya
www.mylifechannels.com
info@mylifechannels.com
973-303-2717

Sonya 2010
Ward

www.SonyaWard.com

DESIGNED BY: URBANVISION.NET